NEW TESTAMENT CROSSWORDS, GALATIANS
IN THE NEW INTERNATIONAL VERSION

JAN DUNCAN-KLIEWER

SENTIA PUBLISHING

Copyright © 2020 by Jan Kliewer

Sentia Publishing Company has the exclusive rights to reproduce this work, to prepare derivative works from this work, to publicly distribute this work, to publicly perform this work, and to publicly display this work.

All rights reserved. No part of this publication may be reproduced, stored in a retrieval system, or transmitted, in any form or by any means, electronic, mechanical, photocopying, recording, or otherwise, without the prior written permission of the copyright owner.

Printed in the United States of America
ISBN 978-1-7340764-8-6

Scriptures are taken from the Holy Bible, New International Version®, NIV®. Copyright© 1973, 1978, 1984, 2011 by Biblia, Inc.™ Used by permission of Zondervan. All rights reserved worldwide. www.zondervan.com

Puzzle clues in bold print with page numbers noted are taken from The Analytical Greek Lexicon Revised 1978 Edition by Harold K. Moulton Copyright© 1977, 1978, 1979 by Zondervan. Used by permission of Zondervan. www.zondervan.com.

All rights reserved. No part of this publication may be reproduced, stored in a retrieval system, or transmitted in any for or by and means without the prior permission of the copyrighted owner.

Printed in the United States of America.

Table of Contents

		Page
About	…………………………	7
Introduction	…………………………	8
Chapter 1	…………………………	10
Chapter 2	…………………………	22
Chapter 3	…………………………	40
Chapter 4	…………………………	56
Chapter 5	…………………………	71
Chapter 6	…………………………	86
Text of Galatians	…………………………	98
Answer Key	…………………………	104

ABOUT JAN

I grew up in a Christian home and in the Independent Christian Church. My dad, a minister, baptized me on April 25, 1971 at Scottsdale Christian Church in Scottsdale, Arizona. I attended Dallas Christian College from 1981 until 1986, graduating with a Secretarial Certificate, an Associate of Applied Science Degree in Secretarial Science, and a Bachelor of Science Degree in Elementary Education. In 2003 I was awarded a Master of Education Degree in Community Counseling from Southwestern Oklahoma State University.

For my tenth birthday I received <u>The Children's Living Bible</u>. At some point I began to read through the entire Bible, which I completed in 1978. However, it is sometimes a struggle for me, and others, to muster enthusiasm for personal Bible reading. This is how the idea for this project emerged—a mode of Bible reading that is interesting and fun, yet meaningful. I believe this idea is a gift from God to me as a way to spend time with His Word, and that blessing is multiplied if it serves others as well.

The book of Galatians is believed to be one of the first books of the New Testament written. When taking courses at DCC in the Greek language, it was exciting to get a more thorough understanding of Scripture by studying the meaning of words from the original Greek text of the New Testament. (Thank you, Dr. Mark Berrier!) This fun and excitement, coupled with the idea of crossword puzzles, developed into this valuable Bible reading experience. Because we will not be able to understand all of the mysteries of God on our own, I recommend praying for the Holy Spirit's influence in understanding His Word.

I want to especially thank my Mom for her many hours of working puzzles to test them out and to proof them for me. I also thank my family and friends for their encouragement. Our hope is that New Testament Crosswords will be used for His Kingdom.

Because of the Lord,

Jan Kliewer

Jan Duncan-Kliewer

ABOUT NTC

NEW TESTAMENT CROSSWORDS (NTC) is an enthusiastic study of the New Testament books of the Bible in crossword puzzle form. It's all about spending time with God's Word! The answers in each puzzle are taken from the New International Version of the New Testament. (**Some editions of the NIV version may differ slightly**.) Clues that appear in bold print are influenced by a study using the original Greek New Testament text. Scripture clues are often cross references of the Galatians content.

This New Testament Crosswords book is a study of the book of Galatians. Each crossword puzzle is designed based on a designated passage and has a correlating fill-in-the-blank puzzle. Each crossword puzzle answer has a place in the fill-in-the-blank puzzle (according to the number of letters in each answer, which is noted below each blank). Through the puzzles, the designated passage of Scripture is completely read and studied, possibly even memorized. The crossword puzzle answer key is located at the back of the book for reference. Enjoy spending time in God's Word...let's get started!

STANDARD APPROACH

1) Use the passage of Scripture in the New International Version of the Bible to complete the fill-in-the-blank puzzle.

2) Complete the crossword puzzle. Answer choices are those words used to complete the fill-in-the-blank puzzle.

3) Check the answer key to verify your puzzle answers.

<u>See the following example from **Romans 1:7**</u>

ACROSS
2 **harmony, tranquility; safety, welfare, health; often with an emphasis on lack of strife or reconciliation in a relation, as when one has "peace with God."**
4 everyone
7 **Male parent**
9 Grace and peace to you from God ___ Father and the Lord Jesus Christ. (I Cor. 1:3)
11 **Joshua, "Yaweh saves"**
13 capital of Italy
14 also
15 **invited**
17 "To Timothy my true son __ the faith…" (I Tim. 1:2)
18 "who have been chosen according to ___ foreknowledge of God the Father…: (I Pet. 1:2)
19 **the one true God**

DOWN
1 "...Grace and peace __ yours in abundance..." (II Pet. 1:2)
3 **Anointed One, Messiah, anointed leader expected to bring in an age of peace and liberty from all oppression; came first to bring liberty from sin.**
5 **dear, the object of special affection and of special relationship**
6 "who through faith ___ shielded by God's power…" (1 Pet. 1:5)
7 **by means of**
8 "neither height nor depth, nor anything else in all creation, will be able __ separate us from the love of God that is in Christ Jesus our Lord. (8:39)
10 **the state of kindness and favor toward someone**
12 **those who are holy (moral quality), consecrated, (ceremonially) acceptable to God**
16 **master; owner**

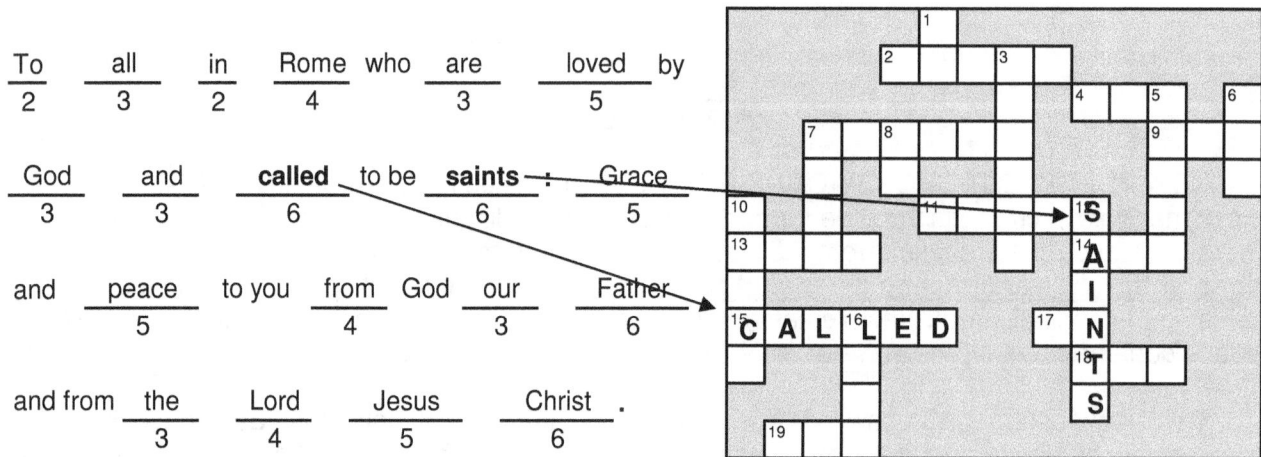

MORE CHALLENGING APPROACH

1) Complete a crossword puzzle. (If you have trouble, then read the New International Version passage and then try again to complete the puzzle.)

2) Check the answer key to verify your puzzle answers.

3) Place each crossword puzzle answer in its correct position in the fill-in-the-blank puzzle.

See the following example from **Romans 1:7**

ACROSS

2 **harmony, tranquility; safety, welfare, health; often with an emphasis on lack of strife or reconciliation in a relation, as when one has "peace with God."**

4 **everyone**

7 **Male parent**

9 Grace and peace to you from God ___ Father and the Lord Jesus Christ. (I Cor. 1:3)

11 **Joshua, "Yaweh saves"**

13 capital of Italy

14 also

15 **invited**

17 "To Timothy my true son ___ the faith..." (I Tim. 1:2)

18 "who have been chosen according to ___ foreknowledge of God the Father...: (I Pet. 1:2)

19 **the one true God**

DOWN

1 "...Grace and peace ___ yours in abundance..." (II Pet. 1:2)

3 **Anointed One, Messiah, anointed leader expected to bring in an age of peace and liberty from all oppression; came first to bring liberty from sin.**

5 **dear, the object of special affection and of special relationship**

6 "who through faith ___ shielded by God's power..." (1 Pet. 1:5)

7 **by means of**

8 "neither height nor depth, nor anything else in all creation, will be able ___ separate us from the love of God that is in Christ Jesus our Lord. (8:39)

10 **the state of kindness and favor toward someone**

12 **those who are holy (moral quality), consecrated, (ceremonially) acceptable to God**

16 **master; owner**

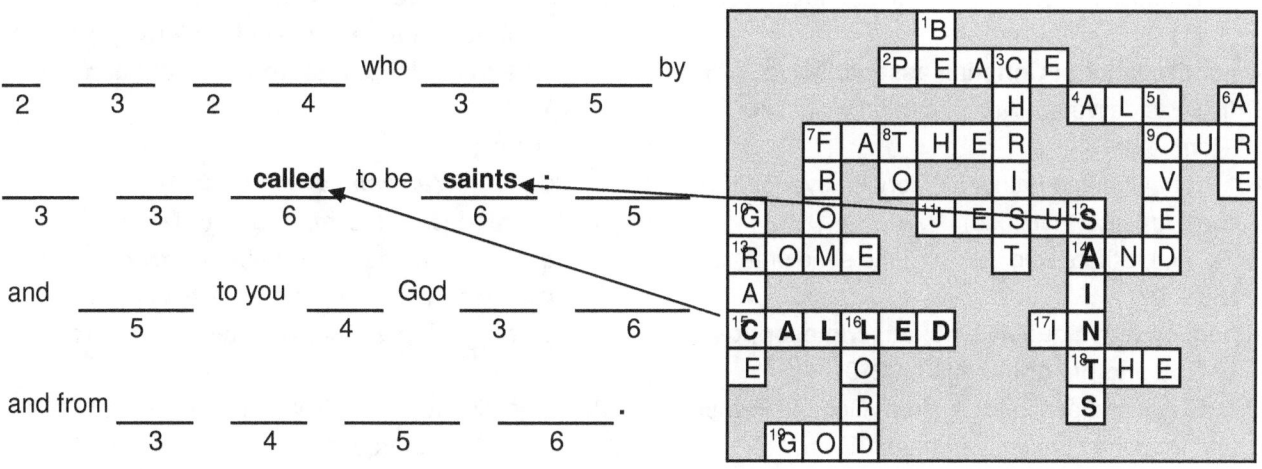

Galatians 1:1-5

ACROSS

1 **Antioch, Iconium, Lystra, and Derbe in north-central Asia Minor (p. 74)**
5 that man (Jesus Christ)
7 "...Where is the philosopher __ this age? Has not God made foolish the wisdom of the world?" (1 Cor. 1:20)
10 yours and mine
11 a human being, a person
12 **fellow countrymen, neighbors; fellow believers in the family of faith; regularly refers to men and women (p. 6)**
14 by means of
16 **time period (p. 186)**
18 *"little;"* **apostle to the Gentiles (p. 313)**, author of Galatians
19 in agreement with, in harmony with (2 words)
22 by means of
24 **eternity (p. 311)**
26 **harmony, tranquility; safety, welfare, health (p. 119)**
27 **wrongdoings; any acts contrary to the will and law of God (p. 17)**
29 "to reveal his Son __ me so that I might preach him among the Gentiles..." (1:16)
30 **the one true God (p. 193)**
31 "...Do what I told the Galatian churches __ do." (1 Cor. 16:1)
33 "I want you to know, brothers, that ___ gospel I preached is not something that man made up." (1:11)
34 **congregations; Christian assemblies (p. 125)**
35 "He was delivered over __ death for our sins..." (Rom. 4:25)
36 "__ our God and Father be glory for ever and ever. Amen." (Phil. 4:20)
37 "...The brothers who are ____ me send greetings." (Phil. 4:21)
38 **bad, negative quality; wicked, crime, opposed to God and his goodness (p. 210)**
39 "...Grace and peace to ___ from God our Father and from the Lord Jesus Christ." (Rom. 1:7)
41 also, even, likewise
42 you and me
43 **decision, desire (p. 156)**
44 "...the Son of Man did not come to be served, but to serve, and to give his life as a ransom ___ many." (Mat. 20:28)
45 myself, I

DOWN

1 **splendor, brilliance, the awesome light that radiates from God's presence associated with his acts of power; honor, praise, speaking of words of excellence and assigning highest status to God (p. 104)**
2 **master (p. 244)**
3 "...it was impossible for death __ keep its hold on him." (Acts 2:24)
4 "Paul, called to be __ apostle of Christ Jesus..." (I Cor. 1:1)
5 him personally
6 human beings, people
8 **male parent or ancestor; an honorific title, leader (p. 312)**
9 and not, neither, not either, not even
13 set free
14 instead
15 "...To him __ the glory forever!" (Rom. 11:36)
17 **kindness and favor toward someone (p. 433)**
18 current, existing
19 **the truth; solemn expression of certainty (p. 18)**
20 **corpse (p. 275)**
21 provided, offered
23 **representative, messenger; divinely appointed founder of the church (p. 47)**
25 **woke from sleep; restored from the dead (p. 112)**
28 in no way
32 **Joshua, *"Yahweh saves"* (p. 200)**
34 **Anointed One, Messiah, Son of David, Jesus who came to bring liberty from sin and peace with God and who will come again to bring all things under his control (p. 439)**
37 "...we also rejoice in God through our Lord Jesus Christ, through ____ we have now received reconciliation." (Rom. 5:11)
40 yours and mine
41 every one of
43 "...God, ___ set me apart from birth..." (1:15)

Galatians 1:1-5

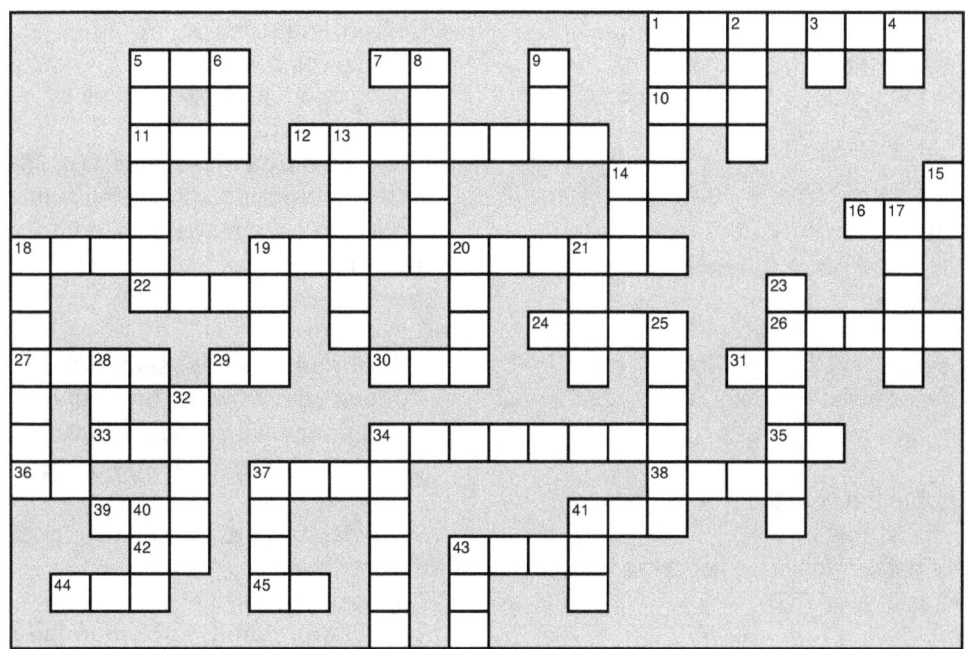

_____ , _____ _____ -- sent _____ _____ _____ _____ _____ a _____ , _____
  4   2   7   3   4   3   3   2   3   3

by _____ _____ _____ _____ _____ _____ , _____ _____ _____
    5   6   3   3   3   6   3   6   3

from the _____ -- and _____ the _____ and sisters _____ _____ , _____ the
          4   3   8   4   2   2

_____ _____ _____ : _____ and _____ _____ _____ from God _____
  8   2   7   5   5   2   3   3

Father, and the _____ Jesus Christ, who _____ _____ _____ _____ _____ _____
                 4   4   7   3   3   4   2

_____ _____ from the _____ _____ _____ , _____ the _____ _____
  6   2   7   4   3   11 (2 words)   4   2

our God and Father, _____ _____ _____ _____ for _____ and ever. _____ .
                      2   4   2   5   4   4

11

Galatians 1:6-9

ACROSS

4 supernatural messenger that serves God
5 "...you distort the words __ the living God..." (Jer. 23:36)
6 someone
9 ought to, must
12 more than one person
14 **proclaim the good news (gospel) (p. 249)**
16 out of
18 actually
20 "And we know that in all things God works for ___ good of those who love him..." (Rom. 8:28)
21 you and I
22 instead
23 "I __ confident in the Lord that you will take no other view..." (5:10)
24 "____ kind of persuasion does not come from the one who calls you." (5:8)
26 by means of
27 "...the gospel I preached to you, _____ you received..." (1 Cor. 15:1)
28 a certain thing (2 words)
29 "...watch out for those who...put obstacles in your way that are contrary to the teaching you ____ learned..." (Rom. 16:17)
30 **cursed (p. 26) (2 words)**
34 **kindness and favor toward someone (p. 433)**
37 on condition that
38 exists
39 "...God works for the good of those ___ love him..." (Rom. 8:28)
42 allow, permit
43 "...They speak visions from their own minds, not from the mouth __ the LORD." (Jer. 23:16)
48 amazed, in wonder, surprised
49 **change (p. 267)**
50 changing from one position to another; abandoning
52 besides (2 words)
54 general term for speaking, tell
56 "...The one who is throwing you ____ confusion will pay the penalty..." (5:10)

DOWN

1 also, even, likewise
2 **good news (p. 172)**
3 "For if someone comes to ___ and preaches a Jesus other than the Jesus we preached..." (2 Cor. 11:4)

DOWN (continued)

4 "Have you been thinking ___ along that we have been defending ourselves to you..." (2 Cor. 12:19)
6 **taken charge of; received (p. 304)**
7 "...If I were still trying to please men, I would not __ a servant of Christ." (1:10)
8 other, dissimilar
9 certain ones
10 in comparison
11 **Anointed One, Messiah, Son of David, Jesus who came to bring liberty from sin and peace with God and who will come again to bring all things under his control (p. 439)**
13 **proclaimed the good news (gospel) (p. 249)**
15 also, likewise
17 in haste, rapidly
19 **told beforehand; spoken in the past (p. 345) (2 words)**
20 **deciding, wanting to; wishing, desiring (p. 192)**
25 "For God, who was at work in the ministry of Peter as __ apostle to the Jews..." (2:8)
30 obviously, apparently
31 at once, immediately
32 bewilderment, disorder
33 not at all
35 **invited, summoned (p. 211)**
36 "For God...was also __ work in my ministry as an apostle to the Gentiles." (2:8)
40 **sky, area above the earth; the place of sun, moon, and stars; place in which God dwells (p. 295)**
41 "...be wise about ____ is good..." (Rom. 16:19)
44 "...What they want __ to alienate you from us..." (4:17)
45 individual
46 you and I
47 like
48 once more
51 "...Do not listen to what the prophets ___ prophesying to you..." (Jer. 23:16)
53 that man, that person
54 "...God...was pleased to reveal his Son in me __ that I might preach him among the Gentiles..." (1:16)
55 "I want you __ know, brothers, that the gospel I preached is not something that man made up." (1:11)

Galatians 1:6-9

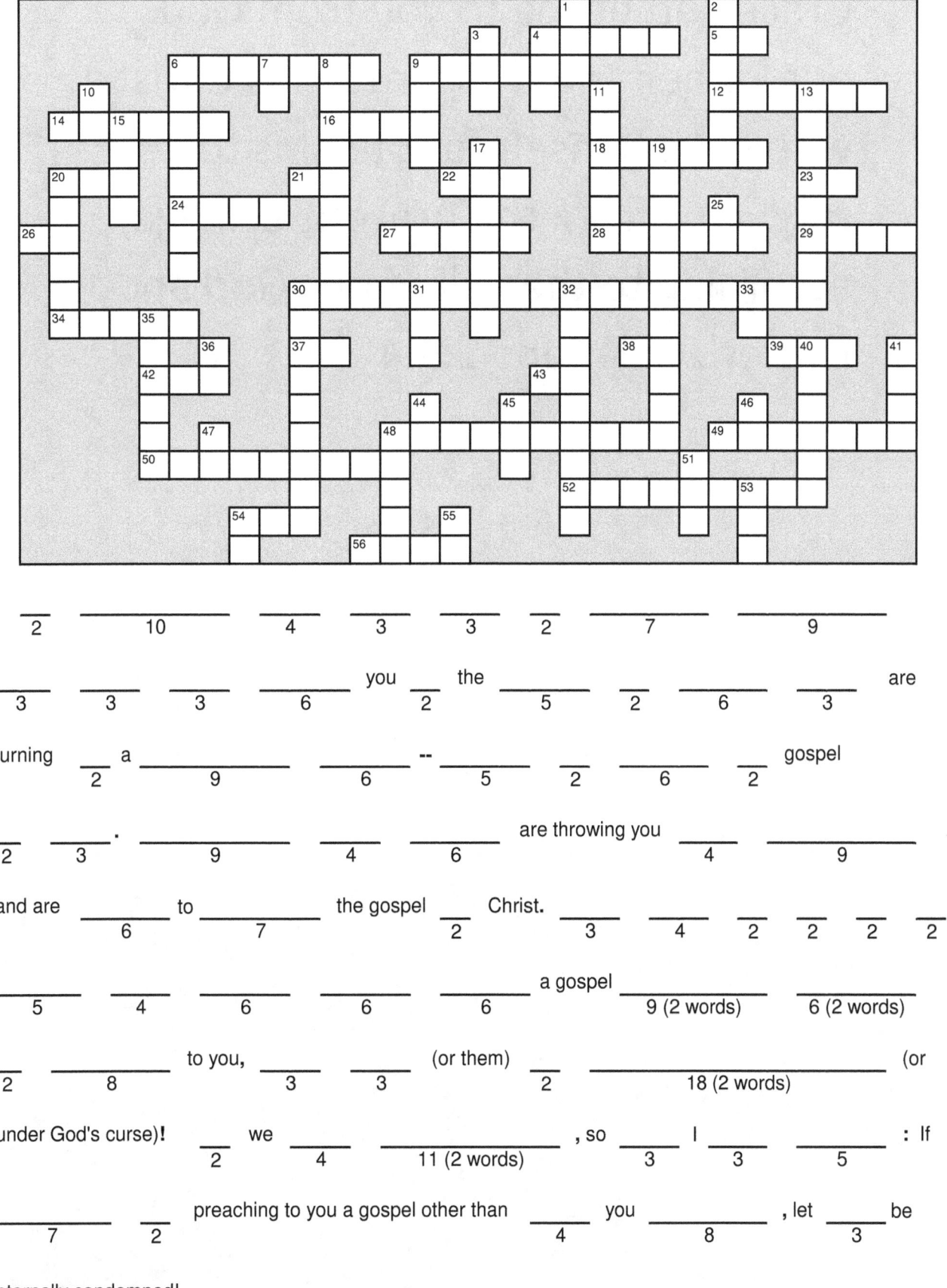

I __ __ __ __ __ __ __ __ __ __ __ __ __ you __ the __ __ __ __ __ __ are
  2   10   4   3   3   2   7   9   3 3 3 6   2   5   2   6   3

turning __ a __ __ __ -- __ __ __ gospel __ __. __ __ __ __ are throwing you __ __
         2   9   6   5   2   6   2   2   3   9   4 6   4   9

and are __ to __ the gospel __ Christ. __ __ __ __ __ __ a gospel __ __
         6   7   2   3   4   2   2   2   2   9 (2 words)   6 (2 words)

__ __ to you, __ __ (or them) __ __ (or
 2   8   3   3   2   18 (2 words)

under God's curse)! __ we __ __ __ , so __ I __ __ : If
                    2   4   11 (2 words)   3   3   5

__ __ preaching to you a gospel other than __ you __ , let __ be
 7   2   4   8   3

eternally condemned!

Grace and peace to you from God our Father and the Lord Jesus Christ, who gave himself for our sins to rescue us from the present evil age, according to the will of our God and Father. Galatians 1:3-4

Galatians 1:10

ACROSS

3 "We ____ not looking for praise from men…" (1 Thes. 2:6)
4 "…by ___ Spirit, not by the written code…" (Rom. 2:29)
5 "I speak the truth in Christ—I __ not lying…" (Rom. 9:1)
8 attempting to satisfy (3 words)
11 **slave (p. 106)**
13 human beings, people
15 "…to see if you _____ stand the test…" (2 Cor. 2:9)

DOWN

1 attempting
2 **Anointed One, Messiah, Son of David, Jesus who came to bring liberty from sin and peace with God and who will come again to bring all things under his control (p. 439)**
5 support, appreciation
6 in comparison
7 exist
8 "…we speak as men approved by God __ be entrusted with the gospel…" (1 Thes. 2:4)
9 "I urge you, brothers, __ watch out for those who cause divisions…" (Rom. 16:17)
10 "But by the grace of God I __ what I am…" (1 Cor. 15:10)
11 yet, again
12 in no way
14 at once, immediately
16 "…circumcision is circumcision __ the heart…" (Rom. 2:29)

___ I _____ _____
 2   3   6

___ win _____ _____
 2   3   8

_____ _____, ___ of God? Or
  2   3   2

___ I _____
 2   14 (3 words)

men (or people)? If I _____
                         4

_____ trying ___ please men, I _____ _____ __ a _____ of
    5   2   5   3   2   7

_____.
    6

Galatians 1:11-12

ACROSS

4 and not, not even
7 **Anointed One, Messiah, Son of David, Jesus who came to bring liberty from sin and peace with God and who will come again to bring all things under his control (p. 439)**
9 understand, be aware of, realize
11 **spoken to publicly, directed, admonished (p. 98)**
13 a human being, a person
15 in no way
16 **Joshua, "*Yahweh saves*" (p. 200)**
17 through
18 **delivered a message about (p. 3)**
20 **making information known (p. 80)**
22 "Now, brothers, I want to remind you of ___ gospel..." (1 Cor. 15:1)
23 prepared
25 took, accepted

DOWN

1 a human being, a person
2 "I assure you before God ____ what I am writing you is no lie." (1:20)
3 the thing
5 but, instead
6 "...I want to remind ___ of the gospel..." (1 Cor. 15:1)
8 a thought
10 desire for, wish for
12 **good news (p. 172)**
14 some, one
17 **fellow countrymen, neighbors; fellow believers in the family of faith; regularly refers to men and women (p. 6)**
19 "...we have testified about God that he raised Christ ____ the dead..." (1 Cor. 15:15)
21 "...the gospel I preached __ you..." (1 Cor. 15:1)
24 "___ the word of God originate with you?..." (1 Cor. 14:36)
26 "As surely as the truth of Christ __ in me..." (2 Cor. 11:10)

Jesus Christ gave Himself to rescue us. Let's not desert Him by turning to anything else, thinking something else could be more important. Let's not be confused by any other message from the world. What is actually important is pleasing God and serving Jesus, God's Son. How do we please God and serve Jesus? By sharing this good message and by loving and serving others. What is God saying to you from Galatians? --Jan

Galatians 1:11-12

I ___ ___ __ ___, ___, ___ ___
   4   3   2   4   8   4   3

___ I ___ ___ ___ that ___
 6   8   2   3   9   3

___ up. I ___ not receive __ ___ ___ ___, ___ was I
 4   3   2   4   3   3   3

___ it; ___, I ___ it __ ___ from
 6   6   8   2   10

___ ___.
 5   6

17

Galatians 1:13-17

ACROSS

1 earlier than, sooner than
4 **originally those belonging to the tribe of Judah, group of people who adhered to the ritual of circumcision (p. 202)**
7 some, one
8 and not, neither
10 **annihilate; to raise havoc (p. 337);** demolish
11 "But Saul began ___ destroy the church..." (Acts 8:3)
14 **religious system held by the Jews; teachings from the law of Moses (p. 202)**
16 at one time, formerly
17 **invited, summoned (p. 211)**
18 certain people
20 visit, meet
21 **child, descendant (p. 413)**
22 right away, instantly
24 the thing (the church of God)
26 out of
28 **same stage of life (p. 390) (2 words)**
31 **devoted (p. 181)**
33 through
34 travel
35 shows purpose or result (2 words)
38 **my mother's womb (p. 234, 269)**
40 **systematically oppressed and harassed a group, pursued, chased (p. 104)**
41 disclose
43 also, even, likewise
44 great or large number of
45 belonging to him (God)
46 "...I appointed you as a prophet ___ the nations." (Jer. 1:5)
47 as soon as
49 separately
52 "...Before I ___ born the LORD called me..." (Isa. 49:1)
53 **the one true God (p. 193)**
54 human, person
55 "We ___ not give in to them..." (Gal.2:5)
56 in the middle of
58 ask advice from
60 "...according to the strictest sect ___ our religion, I lived as a Pharisee." (Acts 26:5)
61 **congregation; Christian assembly (p. 125)**

DOWN

1 above, more than
2 "They have known me ___ a long time..." (Acts 26:5)
3 "I too ___ convinced that I ought to do all that was possible to oppose the name of Jesus of Nazareth." (Acts 26:9)
4 *"foundation of Shalem [peace];"* **King David established this city as his capitol (p. 200)**
5 **conduct (p. 26) (3 words)**
6 "...from the beginning of my life ___ my own country..." (Acts 26:4)
9 **turned back (p. 419),** came back
10 **the capital of Syria (p. 84)**
11 customs
12 "The Jews all know the way I ____ lived ever since I was a child..." (Acts 26:4)
13 **representatives, messengers; divinely appointed founders of the church (p. 47)**
15 opposite of down
19 to what extent
21 put, placed
22 **surpassingly great, most excellent, beyond measure (p. 415)**
23 myself, I
25 "...he ___ formed me in the womb to be his servant..." (Isa. 49:5)
26 **paternal parents; ancestors (p. 312)**
27 may
29 "All those who heard him ____ astonished..." (Acts 9:21)
30 *"desert"* **(p. 50);** large peninsula that borders the Red Sea, Indian Ocean, Persian Gulf, and Syrian Desert
32 afterward
33 however
36 "Do not cause anyone to stumble, whether Jews, Greeks or ___ church of God" (1 Cor. 10:32)
37 **going ahead, going forward (p. 345)**
39 that man (God's Son)
40 delighted
42 to a much greater degree; especially
45 **payed attention to, understood (p. 13)** (2 words)
47 "For God, ___ was at work in the ministry of Peter as an apostle to the Jews..." (Gal. 2:8)
48 also, even, likewise
50 **proclaim the good news (gospel) (p. 172)**
51 "...thousands of Jews have believed, and all of them are zealous for ___ law." (Acts 21:20)
52 left, departed, set off
53 **kindness and favor toward someone (p. 433)**
57 belonging to me
59 in no way

Galatians 1:13-17

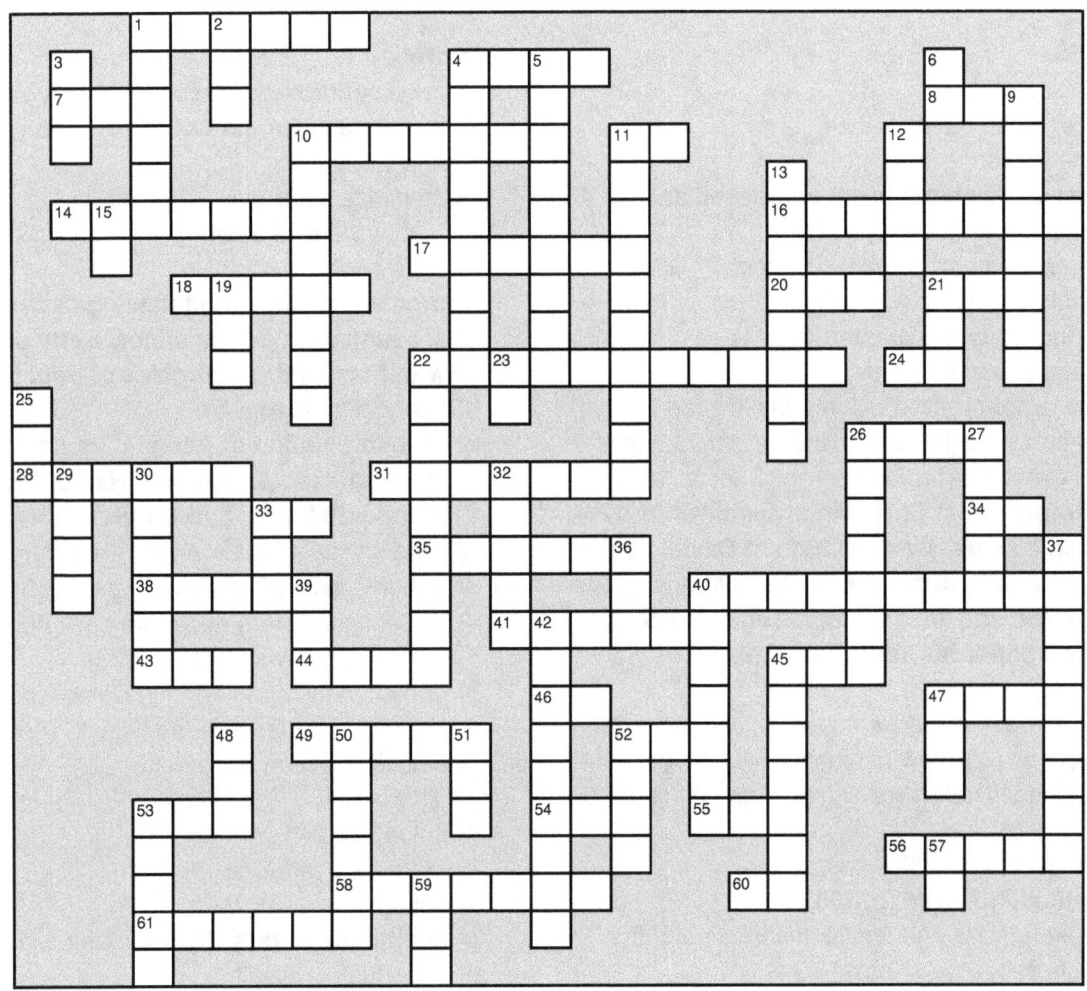

19

Galatians 1:18-24

ACROSS

3 opposite of down
4 merely, just, no more than
7 in the presence of
8 **pursued, systematically oppressed and harassed, chased (p. 104)**
10 "...you, brothers, became imitators __ God's churches in Judea..." (1 Thes. 2:14)
11 **belonging to the master (p. 244)**
13 later, afterward
14 "God, whom I serve with my whole heart in preaching the gospel of his Son, is my witness how constantly I remember ___" (Rom. 1:9)
15 **congregations; Christian assemblies (p. 125)**
16 **Anointed One, Messiah, Son of David, Jesus who came to bring liberty from sin and peace with God and who will come again to bring all things under his control (p. 439)**
19 that man
21 "(...Quirinius ___ governor of Syria.)" (Luke 2:2)
23 "I want you to know, brothers, ____ the gospel I preached is not something that man made up." (1:11)
24 visit, get to know (3 words)
28 **glorified, honored (p. 105)**
29 "Greet Priscilla and Aquila, my fellow workers __ Christ Jesus." (Rom. 16:3)
30 you and me
32 12-month periods of time
34 account, story, information
36 **the one true God (p. 193)**
37 24-hour periods of time
40 "...the Jews conspired __ kill him," (Acts 9:23)
41 once, at one time
43 "...to confirm by word of mouth ____ we are writing." (Acts 15:27)
44 thirteen, fourteen, _____
45 "...the churches of the Gentiles ___ grateful to them." (Rom. 16:4)
46 among
48 **"foundation of Shalem [peace];" King David established this city as his capitol (p. 200)**
50 **payed attention, understood, obeyed (p. 13)**
52 male adult person
54 attempted
55 observed, visited with

DOWN

1 **representatives, messengers; divinely appointed founders of the church (p. 47)**
2 not, not at all
5 then, afterward
6 "...they were all afraid __ him..." (Acts 9:26)
7 male sibling
8 **proclaiming the good news (gospel) (p. 172)**
9 **A country in SE Asia Minor, a city of which was Tarsus, the birthplace of Paul (p. 231)**
10 at one time, formerly
12 **An abbreviation of Assyria; its chief cities were Damascus, Antioch, Hama, Biblos, Aleppo, Palmyra, and Carchemish (p. 392)**
17 "The words of the prophets are in agreement with this, as it __ written:" (Acts 15:15)
18 "...Saul grew more and more powerful and baffled ___ Jews..." (Acts 9:22)
20 "...baffled the Jews living in Damascus by proving ____ Jesus is the Christ." (Acts 9:22)
21 putting in a form to be read
22 different
23 those people
25 promise, guarantee
26 not any
27 **annihilate; to raise havoc; demolish (p. 337)**
28 individually, myself
31 **the land that belonged to the Jews (tribe of Judah) (p. 202)**
33 remained
35 **Cephas, "*rock*," one of Jesus' disciples (p. 231)**
38 "...I __ an Israelite myself..." (Rom. 11:1)
39 following, subsequent to
41 **trust, the Christian system of belief and lifestyle (p. 314)**
42 untruth
43 traveled
45 also, even, likewise
46 "All those ___ heard him were astonished..." (Acts 9:21)
47 that man
48 **"*follower, replacer, one who follows the heel,*" (p. 198);** *one of Jesus' brothers*
49 myself, I
51 also, even, likewise
53 presently, currently
54 "...Saul grew more and more powerful and baffled ___ Jews..." (Acts 9:22)

Galatians 1:18-24

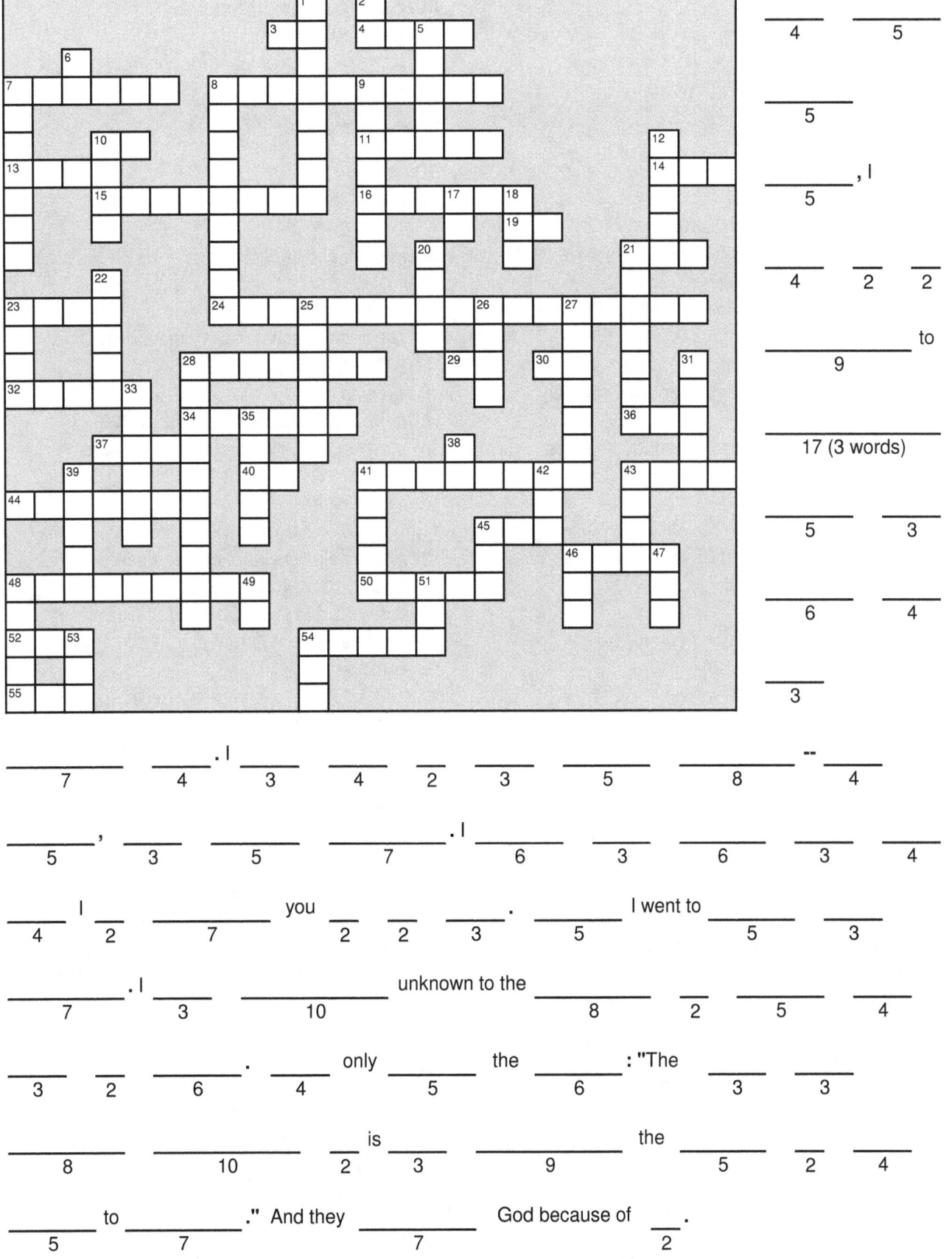

Galatians 2:1-5

ACROSS

1. ten plus four
6. **steal in (p. 307);** watch, work undercover
7. **yield, submit (p. 117)** (2 words)
10. positions, stations
13. that man
15. smooth, flat, level
16. in the middle of, amid
18. **strived, given effort (p. 409)**
20. **a convert, friend, and helper of Paul (p. 406)**
21. **Joshua, "*Yahweh saves*" (200)**
22. **pagans; foreign nation (p. 116),** people who are not Jews
23. you and I
24. **proclaim the good news (gospel) (p. 230)**
26. but, instead
28. fake, untrue, or misleading friends (2 words)
32. next to, beside
35. likewise
37. reply, answer
39. **striving, giving effort (p. 409);** going fast on your two legs and feet
41. belonging to me
44. "...wonders God ___ done among the Gentiles..." (Acts 15:12)
45. **reported to (p. 26)** (2 words)
46. "...so that I might live ___ God." (2:19)
47. hold, keep
48. afterward
50. however
52. "The reason I wrote you ___ to see if you would stand the test and be obedient in everything." (2 Cor. 2:9)
55. "Even though I may not ___ an apostle to others, surely I am to you!" (1 Cor. 9:2)
56. had the surgical process done that was originally the sign of the covenant between Abraham and God
57. **forced (p. 21)**
58. subject, issue; trouble, problem
60. "...No one claimed ____ any of his possessions was his own..." (Acts 4:32)
62. a number of

ACROSS (continued)

64. appeared, looked
66. "...I ___ not run or labor for nothing." (Phil. 2:16)
67. small portion of time

DOWN

1. "I do all this ___ the sake of the gospel..." (1 Cor. 9:23)
2. brought, accompanied
3. in no way
4. opposite of down
5. "I have been constantly ___ the move..." (2 Cor. 11:26)
6. servants
8. **ineffective, useless, foolish (p. 228)**
9. "...even _____ we are Roman citizens..." (Acts 16:37)
10. stay constantly
11. "___ I say, live by the Spirit..." (5:16)
12. "All the believers were one ___ heart and mind..." (Acts 4:32)
14. **reality (p. 15)**
17. **good news (p. 172)**
19. you and me
20. "...found that ___ Lord had opened a door for me," (2 Cor. 2:12)
21. **"*foundation of Shalem [peace];*" King David established this city as his capitol (p. 200)**
23. in the company of
25. "...truth ___ the gospel..." (2:14)
26. periods of 12 months
27. "...Paul and Barnabas were appointed...to see the apostles and elders about ____ question." (Acts 15:2)
29. **"*son of comfort*" (p. 66);** called to work with Paul
30. "When they came ___ Jerusalem, they were welcomed by the church..." (Acts 15:4)
31. "...it ___ distributed to anyone as he had need." (Acts 4:35)
33. persons in charge, directors
34. **Gentile, a class of person distinguished from the Jewish race and nation (p. 133)**

Galatians 2:1-5

DOWN (Continued)
36 "...I did not run __ labor for nothing." (Phil. 2:16)
38 not publicly
40 **came in secretly, snuck in (p. 307)**
42 "___, my brothers, were called to be free…" (5:13)
43 "...we should not make it difficult for the Gentiles ___ are turning to God." (Acts 15:19)
46 **liberty, not being enslaved (p. 132)**
49 contest, competition, pursuit
50 for the reason that
51 occasion, instance
53 also, even, likewise
54 left, travelled
56 **Anointed One, Messiah, Son of David, Jesus who came to bring liberty from sin and peace with God and who will come again to bring all things under his control (p. 439)**
59 those people
61 also
63 yours and mine
65 myself, I

Know that a man is not justified by observing the law, but by faith in Jesus Christ. So we, too, have put our faith in Christ Jesus that we may be justified by faith in Christ and not by observing the law, because by observing the law no one will be justified. Galatians 2:16

Galatians 2:1-5

_____ _____ _____ I _____ _____ again _____
    8   5   5   4   2   2

_____, _____ _____ _____ _____. I _____
    9   4   4   4   8   4

_____ _____ _____. I went _____ _____ to a revelation _____
   5   5   4   2   8   3

_____ _____ _____ _____ _____ I _____
9 (2 words)   4   3   6   4   6

_____ the _____. _____ I _____ this _____ to those
  5   8   3   3   9

_____ _____ to _____ _____, _____ fear that I _____
 3   6   2   7   3   3

_____ _____ _____ _____ _____ in _____. _____
  7   2   3   3   2   4   4   3

_____ _____ Titus, who _____ with _____, was _____ to be
 3   4   3   2   9

_____, even _____ _____ was a _____. This _____
   11   6   2   5   6

arose _____ _____ _____ had _____
       7   4   13 (2 words)   11

_____ _____ to _____ the _____ _____ in _____
 3   5   3   2   7   2   4

_____ _____ _____ to make _____ _____. We did not
  6   5   3   2   6

_____ to them _____ a _____, _____ that the _____ _____ the gospel
6 (2 words)   3   6   2   5   2

might _____ with _____.
       6   3

Galatians 2:6-10

ACROSS

- 4 knew, understood
- 7 *"son of comfort"* **(p. 66)**; called to work with Paul
- 9 exact
- 11 those people
- 12 people
- 14 "I opposed him to his face, because he ___ clearly in the wrong." (2:11)
- 15 "...take pride in himself, without comparing himself ___ somebody else," (6:4)
- 16 others and I
- 17 **making every effort, doing one's best (p. 373)**
- 20 **producing with energy (p. 139)** (3 words)
- 21 **people not circumcised or of the Mosaic covenant (p. 14)**
- 22 "Let us not become weary in doing good, ___ at the proper time we will reap a harvest if we do not give up." (6:9)
- 23 **think of (p. 270)**
- 26 "...we speak ___ men approved by God..." (1 Thes. 2:4)
- 27 "...I will repay each of you according ___ your deeds." (Rev. 2:23)
- 28 "With great power the apostles continued to testify to the resurrection of the Lord Jesus, and much grace was upon them ___." (Acts 4:33)
- 29 "Paul, ___ apostle of Christ Jesus by the command of God our Savior..." (1 Tim. 1:1)
- 30 **originally those belonging to the tribe of Judah, group of people who adhered to the ritual of circumcision (p. 322)**
- 31 "...some false brothers ___ infiltrated our ranks..." (2:4)
- 32 in no way
- 33 **leaders (p. 378)**
- 35 also, even, likewise
- 36 **representative, messenger; divinely appointed founder of the church (p. 47)**
- 38 causes, achieves
- 39 "...his grace ___ me was not without effect..." (I Cor. 15:10)
- 40 "We ___ not looking for praise from men..." (1 Thes. 2:6)
- 42 **proclaiming, lecturing, speaking (p. 314)**
- 46 but, quite the opposite (3 words)
- 50 **Cephas, "*rock*" (p. 323)**; one of Jesus' disciples
- 52 "...not I, but the grace of God ___ was with me." (1 Cor. 15:10)
- 54 significant, valuable
- 56 *"Yahweh is gracious;"* **brother of James the apostle (p. 205)**
- 57 provided, offered
- 58 enhanced, improved
- 59 practice, perform
- 61 not any
- 62 change, modification

DOWN

- 1 also, even, likewise
- 2 "I went ___ response to a revelation..." (2:2)
- 3 like
- 5 go on, persist
- 6 "That kind of persuasion ___ not come from the one who calls you." (5:8)
- 7 "___ her teaching she misleads my servants..." (Rev. 2:20)
- 8 "...we speak as men approved by God to ___ entrusted with the gospel..." (1 Thes. 2:4)
- 10 outer
- 11 job, chore, duty
- 12 myself, I
- 13 **noticed; perceived (p. 291)**
- 16 production; labor
- 17 handed, assigned (2 words)
- 18 **the one true God (p. 193)**
- 19 likewise; in addition
- 20 had the same opinion
- 21 **good news (p. 172)**
- 22 **close association between persons, emphasizing what is common between them (p. 234)**
- 24 communication, meaning
- 25 "...the world has ___ crucified to me, and I to the world." (6:14)
- 29 look
- 30 *"follower, replacer, one who follows the heel,"* **one of the twelve apostles along with his brother John (p. 198)**
- 34 requested
- 36 "___ once he began to preach in the synagogues that Jesus is the Son of God." (Acts 9:20)
- 37 **people of few resources, culturally considered oppressed, despised, and miserable (p. 356)**
- 41 "...all the churches will know that I am he ___ searches hearts and minds..." (Rev. 2:23)
- 43 **a sign of friendship, trust, and covenant (p. 87)** (2 words)
- 44 travel, reach
- 45 belonging to me
- 47 not anything
- 48 "that conforms to ___ glorious gospel of the blessed God, which he entrusted to me." (1 Tim. 1:11)
- 49 ought to, must
- 51 **thought, considered, regarded, an action of the mind and heart for processing information into understanding and choices (p. 104)**
- 53 provided, offered
- 55 certain people
- 56 estimate, consider
- 57 **kindness and favor toward someone (p. 433)**
- 60 "...with the help ___ our God we dared to tell you his gospel..." (1 Thes. 2:2)

Galatians 2:6-10

_____ seemed _____ -- whatever
 2   3   5   3   2   2   9   4   4

_____ ; _____
 5   2   10   2   2   3   4   3   5   2

_____ -- those _____
 8   10   3   5   7   2   2

_____ . _____ , they _____ I _____
  7   13 (3 words)   3   4   3   4

_____ the _____ to the
13 (2 words)   3   4   2   9   6

27

I have been crucified with Christ and I no longer live, but Christ lives in me. The life I live in the body, I live by faith in the Son of God, who loved me and gave himself for me.
Galatians 2:20

Galatians 2:6-10

_____, just as _____ had been to the _____. For God, who ____ _____ the
   8   5   4   3   8 (3 words)

ministry of Peter __ __ _____ to the Jews, was ____ ___ ____ __ my
                         2 2   7   4 2 4 2

ministry as an apostle to the Gentiles. _____, Peter ____ ____, those _____ to be
                                                5   3   4   7

_____, ___ me ___ _____ the _____ of _____ when
  7   4   3   8   9 (2 words)   10

they _____ the ___ _____ to me. They ___ that __ __ __
      10   5   5   6   2 6 2

to the Gentiles, and they to the Jews. ___ they _____ was that we should _____ __
                                       3   5   8 2

_____ the ___, the ___ thing I was ___ to __.
   8   4   4   5 2

Circumcision is a sign of the covenant between Abraham and God. Abraham's grandson, Jacob, was later renamed Isreal by God. This circumcision covenant continued between God and Abraham's descendants, the Isrealites. I remember from Bible College that circumcision also probably provides some amount of protection from certain infections and cancer. Most likely it was commanded to be carried out on the eighth day after birth since the level of blood clotting is higher that day to help stop bleeding. What is God saying to you from Galatians? --Jan

Galatians 2:11-13

ACROSS

1 him personally
5 those people
6 assembly, crowd, sort
8 away, withdrawn
10 "...You went into ___ house of uncircumcised men and ate with them." (Acts 11:3)
11 **Cephas, "*rock*" (p. 231);** one of Jesus' disciples
12 particular, specific
13 arrived
15 that man
18 came, got here
22 "...Do not call anything impure ____ God has made clean." (Acts 11:9)
24 **condemned, convicted (p. 215)** (4 words)
28 "...who ___ I to think that I could oppose God?" (Acts 11:17)
29 was accustomed or familiar
32 linked up with
34 people who are decendants of Jacob
35 **alarmed (p. 428),** scared
37 at the time
38 was the capital of Syria; city with the first Gentile church
39 fit in, were from
40 through, as a result of

DOWN

1 insincerity, double standards
2 consume, have a meal
3 "...I had been entrusted with the task of preaching the gospel __ the Gentiles, just as Peter had been to the Jews." (2:7)
4 **resisted, rebelled, withstood (p. 30)**
5 belonging to them
7 by means of
8 for the reason that
9 originally the sign of the covenant between Abraham and God
14 guys, males
15 that man
16 move, pull
17 also, likewise
19 "The circumcised believers who had come with Peter were astonished that ___ gift of the Holy Spirit had been poured out even on the Gentiles." (Acts 10:45)
20 that man
21 additional
23 certain people or men
25 **guided away; carried off to associate with the lowly (p. 386)** (2 words)
26 "Now those who had been scattered by the persecution __ connection with Stephen traveled as far as Phoenicia, Cyprus and Antioch..." (Acts 11:19)
27 **pagans; foreign nation, people who are not Jews (p. 116)**
28 among
30 "__ when Peter went up to Jerusalem, the circumcised believers criticized him" (Acts 11:2)
31 belonging to him
33 "...the Gentiles also had received the word __ God." (Acts 11:1)
34 *"follower, replacer, one who follows the heel,"* **one of the twelve apostles along with his brother John (p. 198)**
36 **in someone's presence or sight (p. 353)**
38 also, even, likewise
39 however, on the contrary

Galatians 2:11-13

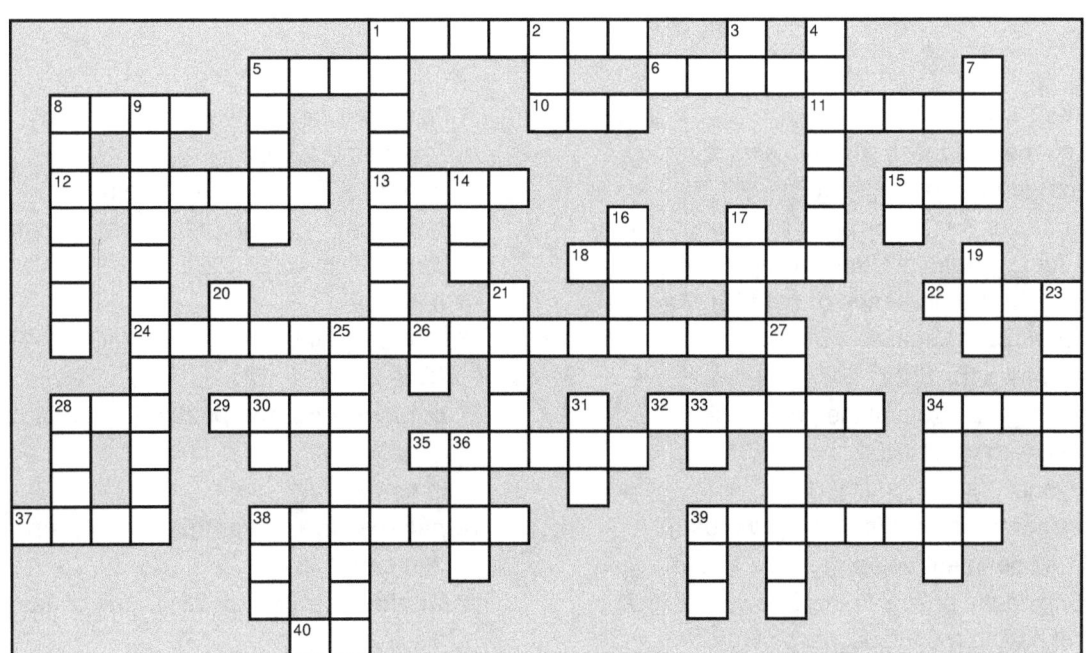

___ ___ ___ ___ ___, I ___ ___ to ___ ___,
 4   5   4   2   7   7   3   3   4

___ ___ ___ _____. Before ___ ___ came
 7   2   3   17 (4 words)   7   3

___ ___, ___ to ___ ___ ___ ___ ___. ___ when ___
 4   5   2   4   3   4   3   8   3   4

_____, he began to ___ ___ ___ separate ___ from ___ Gentiles
     7   4   4   3   7   3

because he was ___ ___ ___ who ___ to the _____
                6   2   5   8   12

___. The ___ ___ ___ him ___ his ___, ___ ___ ___
 5   5   4   6   2   9   2   4   2

___ hypocrisy ___ Barnabas was ___.
 5   4   9

Galatians 2:14

ACROSS

3 **reality (p. 15)**
4 "...take note of those who live according to the pattern we gave ___." (Php. 3:17)
5 "...whatever was to my profit I now consider loss for ___ sake of Christ." (Php. 3:8)
8 **before, in the presence of (p. 136)** (3 words)
11 **compel (p. 21),** make
12 **good news (p. 172)**
14 "...so ____ the truth of the gospel might remain with you." (2:5)
15 everyone
17 **in a pagan manner (p. 116)** (3 words)
18 "...I had been entrusted ____ the task of preaching the gospel to the Gentiles…" (2:7)
21 "...not having a righteousness of my own ____ comes from the law…" (Php. 3:9)
22 characteristics of descendants of Jacob
23 exist
24 **noticed; perceived (p. 291)**
26 traditions, routines, habits
28 at the time
29 "...the ministry of Peter as an apostle __ the Jews…" (2:8)
30 those people
31 also, even, likewise

DOWN

1 "...those who believe ___ children of Abraham." (Gal. 3:7)
2 after that, in that case, therefore
3 "...so that ___ truth of the gospel might remain with you." (2:5)
4 however
6 "...I live by faith in the Son __ God…" (Gal. 2:20)
7 **behaving rightly (p. 292)** (3 words)
9 go along with
10 in no way
12 **pagans; foreign nation, people who are not Jews (p. 116)**
13 **Cephas, "*rock*" (p. 231),** one of Jesus' disciples
16 **in a Jewish manner (p. 202)** (3 words)
19 in what way? (3 words)
20 those people
21 "We did not give in __ them for a moment, so that the truth of the gospel might remain with you." (2:5)
25 "...If I ____ still trying to please men, I would not be a servant of Christ." (1:10)
27 general term for speaking

The new covenant through Jesus Christ provided by His death, burial, and resurrection outdoes the old covenant of circumcision. However, Jews (sometimes interchangeable with Israelites) continued to obey the practice of circumcision. Since circumcision provides health benefits, it is still a good practice for Jews and non-Jews. But, it should not be forced religiously on those who are not Jews to obey the practice. Some of Jesus' followers seemed to be confused about these things at first. What is God saying to you from Galatians? --Jan

Galatians 2:14

___ I ___ ___ ___ ___ ___ ___
 4   3   4   4   4   3   12 (3 words)

___ ___ ___ ___ ___ ___ , I ___ ___
 4   3   5   2   3   6   4   2

___ _____ ___ ___ ," ___ ___ a Jew,
 5   9 (3 words)   4   3   3   3

___ you ___ _____ ___ not _____ .
 3   4   12 (3 words)   3   8 (3 words)

_____ , ___ , ___ you ___ ___ ___
 7 (3 words)   4   4   5   8   2

___ ___ ___ ?
 6   6   7

Galatians 2:15-16

ACROSS

1 "...the one who justifies those who have faith __ Jesus." (Rom. 3:26)
3 "...no one will __ declared righteous in his sight by observing the law..." (Rom. 3:20)
5 "All of us who ___ mature should take such a view of things..." (Php. 3:15)
6 also
8 **Anointed One, Messiah, Son of David, Jesus who came to bring liberty from sin and peace with God and who will come again to bring all things under his control (p. 439)**
10 people who are decendants of Jacob
13 consequently, therefore
15 **working (p. 165);** abiding by, respecting, following, complying with
18 in no way
19 human being, person
21 **trust, the Christian system of belief and lifestyle (p. 314)**
22 not any
23 "...we who worship __ the Spirit of God..." (Php. 3:3)
25 **regulations, principles; the first five books of the Scriptures, or any single command of the Scriptures (p. 279)**
26 also, even, likewise
27 "For we maintain ____ a man is justified by faith..." (Rom. 3:28)
28 you and I

DOWN

2 in no way
3 since; for the reason that
4 **Joshua, "*Yahweh saves*" (p. 200)**
7 single person
9 "Where, then, __ boasting? It is excluded..." (Rom. 3:27)
10 **vindicated, declared righteous, in a proper relationship with God (p. 102)**
11 "For it is we ___ are the circumcision..." (Php. 3:3)
12 "...We ____ been saying that Abraham's faith was credited to him as righteousness." (Rom. 4:9)
14 "...our citizenship is __ heaven..." (Php. 3:20)
16 **nature (p. 432);** beginning, origin
17 **pagan; foreign nation, people who are not Jews (p. 116)**
19 "...I have lost all things. I consider them rubbish, that I ___ gain Christ" (Php. 3:8)
20 **possess information; recognize, realize; understand (p. 283)**
23 "___ whatever was to my profit I now consider loss for the sake of Christ." (Php. 3:7)
24 "...man is justified by faith apart from observing ___ law." (Rom. 3:28)

Since Gentiles (non-Jews) generally did not know the one true God, they seemed to be referred to as sinners. Of course, both Gentiles and Jews are sinners. But all Gentiles and Jews can be saved through the new covenant, which is belief in the death, burial, and resurrection of Jesus Christ, God's Son. --Jan

Galatians 2:15-16

___ ___ ___ ___ ___ ___ ___ ___
 2   3   3   4   2   5   3   3

_____ sinners' ___ a ___ ___ ___
     7   4   3   2   3

_____ by _____ ___ ___ , ___ by ___
     9   9   3   3   3   5

___ _____ _____ . we, ___ , ___ put our faith ___ Christ Jesus
 2   5   6   2   3   4   2

that we ___ ___ justified by faith in Christ and not by observing the law, _____
         3   2   7

by observing the law ___ ___ will be justified.
                      2   3

Galatians 2:17-21

ACROSS

5 **in vain, to no purpose (p. 98)** (2 words)
7 turns out to be
9 difinitely, certainly
12 **commend, recommend; demonstrate consistency, bring out (p. 391)**
14 **child, descendant (p. 413)**
17 **regulation, principle; first five books of the Scriptures, or any single command of the Scriptures (p. 279)**
18 "...we ____ been united with him like this in his death..." (Rom. 6:5)
19 rather
20 I myself
21 I myself
22 "...he died to sin once ____ all..." (Rom. 6:10)
24 "...if anyone ____ not have the Spirit of Christ, he does not belong to Christ." (Rom. 8:9)
25 also
26 "...he ____ raised Christ from the dead will also give life to your mortal bodies..." (Rom. 8:11)
27 "...you also died ____ the law through the body of Christ..." (Rom. 7:4)
28 "...If God is for us, who can ____ against us?" (Rom. 8:31)
29 **look; try to obtain, desire to possess, strive (p. 182)**
30 **vindicated, declared righteous, in a proper relationship with God (p. 102)**
32 "Therefore ____ not let sin reign in your mortal body..." (Rom. 6:12)
33 "...our old self was crucified with him so that ____ body of sin might be done away with..." (Rom. 6:6)
34 **what is right, justice, doing what is in agreement with God's standards, being in proper relationship with God (p. 102)**
35 could
37 "...sin shall not be your master, because you ____ not under law, but under grace." (Rom. 6:14)
38 **those with moral failure, those violating God's will or law (p. 17)**
41 "...____ we are is plain to God..." (2 Cor. 5:11)
43 "We were therefore buried ____ him through baptism into death..." (Rom. 6:4)
44 put to death by nailing to a cross
45 **flesh, human structure (p. 363)**
46 not again, not any more, no further (2 words)
48 achieved, acquired, obtained
50 is devoted to, cared for
51 we personally

DOWN

1 "...do not let sin reign ____ your mortal body so that you obey its evil desires." (Rom. 6:12)
2 that thing
3 in order to (2 words)
4 "What a wretched man I ____!" (Rom. 7:24)
5 **trust, the Christian system of belief and lifestyle (p. 314)**
6 **handed over, betrayed, delivered to prison; entrusted, committed (p. 302)**
7 "We live ____ faith, not by sight." (2 Cor. 5:7)
8 **wrongdoing; any act contrary to the will and law of God (p. 17)**
10 "...that we should no longer ____ slaves to sin..." (Rom. 6:6)
11 **transgressor (p. 300)**
12 **serves, ministers to, helps (p. 92)**; encourages, elevates, advertises
13 him personally
15 "...if Christ is in you...your spirit is alive because ____ righteousness." (Rom. 8:10)
16 **found, discovered (p. 176)**
17 existence, being
23 "...we know ____ our old self was crucified with him..." (Rom. 6:6)
24 expired, passed away, departed
27 "...you also died to the law _____ the body of Christ..." (Rom. 7:4)
28 "...anyone who has died has ____ freed from sin." (Rom. 6:7)
31 **reject (p. 8)** (2 words)
32 **thrown down, abolished (p. 218)**
35 signify, indicate, imply, suggest
36 **kindness and favor toward someone (p. 433)**
39 in no way
40 develop, put together, or encourage again

Galatians 2:17-21

DOWN (Continued)

41 at the same time as
42 "...I would not have known what coveting really was __ the law had not said, "Do not covet." (Rom. 7:7)
43 you and I
44 **Anointed One, Messiah, Son of David, Jesus who came to bring liberty from sin and peace with God and who will come again to bring all things under his control (p. 439)**
47 exists, resides, stays
48 **the one true God (p. 193)**
49 "...there is now no condemnation ___ those who are in Christ Jesus" (Rom. 8:1)
50 exist, reside, stay
51 "...those who are led by the Spirit __ God are sons of God." (Rom. 8:14)

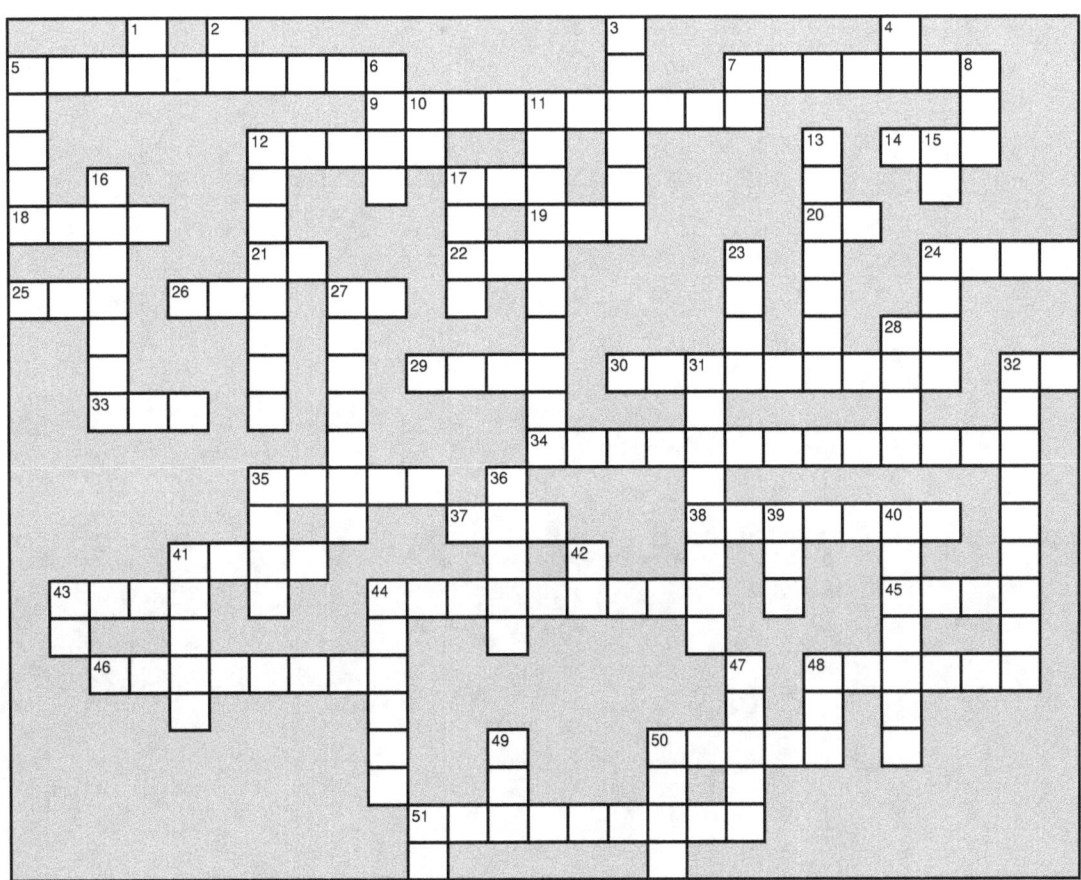

I do not set aside the grace of God, for if righteousness could be gained through the law, Christ died for nothing! Galatians 2:21

Galatians 2:17-21

____ (2), ____ (5) ____ (2) ____ (4) ____ (2) ____ (2) ____ (9) ____ (2) ____ (6), ____ (2)

____ (7) ____ (7) ____ (4) we ____ (9) ____ (3) ____ (7), ____ (4) that

____ (4) that Christ ____ (8) ____ (3)? ____ (10) ____ (3)! If I ____ (7) ____ (4) I

____ (9), I ____ (5) that I ____ (2) a ____ (10). ____ (3) ____ (7) ____ (3) ____ (3)

I ____ (4) to the law ____ (6 (2 words)) I ____ (5) ____ (4) for ____ (3). I ____ (4) ____ (4)

____ (9) ____ (4) Christ ____ (3) I ____ (8 (2 words)) live, ____ (3) Christ ____ (5) in ____ (2). The

____ (4) I live in the ____ (4), I live ____ (2) ____ (5) in the ____ (3) ____ (2) God, ____ (3) ____ (5) ____ (2)

and ____ (4) ____ (7) ____ (3) me. I ____ (2) not ____ (8 (2 words)) the ____ (5) ____ (2) God, for

if ____ (13) could ____ (2) ____ (6) through the law, Christ died ____ (10 (2 words))!

Although I believe God leads us to do good works of service, it is not good works that save us. Loving God and loving others is what is important. With this love, we are saved by belief in the death, burial, and resurrection of Jesus Christ, God's Son. It is amazing that Jesus offered Himself willingly as a sacrifice to save all sinners. It is by faith in Jesus that we can accept this precious gift of salvation by which we can spend eternity in Heaven. What is God saying to you from Galatians? --Jan

Galatians 3:1-5

ACROSS

1 in comparison
4 **the one true God (p. 193)**
5 God the Holy Ghost, Wind, or Breath
8 also, even, likewise
9 the thing, the purpose
10 **faith in, faithfulness to, trusting (p. 314)**
12 in the midst of
13 "How foolish ___ are, and how slow of heart to believe…" (Luke 24:25)
14 **in vain, to no purpose (p. 98)** (2 words)
18 "…In the name of Jesus Christ I command ___ to come out of her!" (Acts 16:18)
19 without a doubt, plainly, unmistakably
21 **study, be instructed (p. 257)**
22 a single, an individual
23 **organs of sight; mental perception and understanding (p. 291)**
24 experienced, endured unpleasant experiences
26 "Did not the Christ have ___ suffer these things and then enter his glory?" (Luke 24:26)
28 actual, exact
29 attempting, struggling, making an effort
30 since, on condition that
31 detail, point, idea
33 **no purpose (p. 98)**
36 **flesh, body, opposite of spiritual (p. 363)**
39 "Christ is the end of the law ___ that there may be righteousness for everyone who believes." (Rom. 10:4)
40 **cast a spell over (p. 67)**
41 **supernatural powers and abilities (p. 107)**
44 "…Their hearts ___ always going astray, and they have not known my ways." (Heb. 3:10)
45 abide by, respect, follow
47 senseless
49 "…he learned obedience from ____ he suffered" (Heb. 5:8)
50 "they had seen a vision of angels, who said he ___ alive." (Luke 24:23)
51 "…he was the one ___ was going to redeem Israel…" (Luke 24:21)

DOWN

2 emphatically, indeed, surely
3 in the role of, having the status of, being
4 **supply (p. 163)**
6 **written about beforehand; advertised, proclaimed (p. 342)**
7 "…Who cut in on you and kept you from obeying ___ truth?" (5:7)
8 reach, achieve, accomplish
10 making a start
11 belonging to you
14 "___ we also have had the gospel preached to us, just as they did…" (Heb. 4:2)
15 abiding by, respecting, following
16 "He is not here; he ___ risen…" (Luke 24:6)
17 **people "from Galatia" (p. 74)**
19 put to death by being nailed to a cross
20 endeavor; struggle, energy, strength
25 from
27 by means of
32 "How, then, can they call on the one they ____ not believed in?" (Rom. 10:14)
34 listened to, paid attention to, were told
35 objective, aim, target
36 belonging to Him, belonging to God
37 at the present time
38 take
40 facing, ahead of
41 greatly, long
42 **Anointed One, Messiah, Son of David, Jesus who came to bring liberty from sin and peace with God and who will come again to bring all things under his control (p. 439)**
43 following, subsequent to
46 "…What Israel sought ___ earnestly it did not obtain…" (Rom. 11:7)
48 **regulations, principles; the first five books of the Scriptures, or any single command of the Scriptures (p. 279)**

Galatians 3:1-5

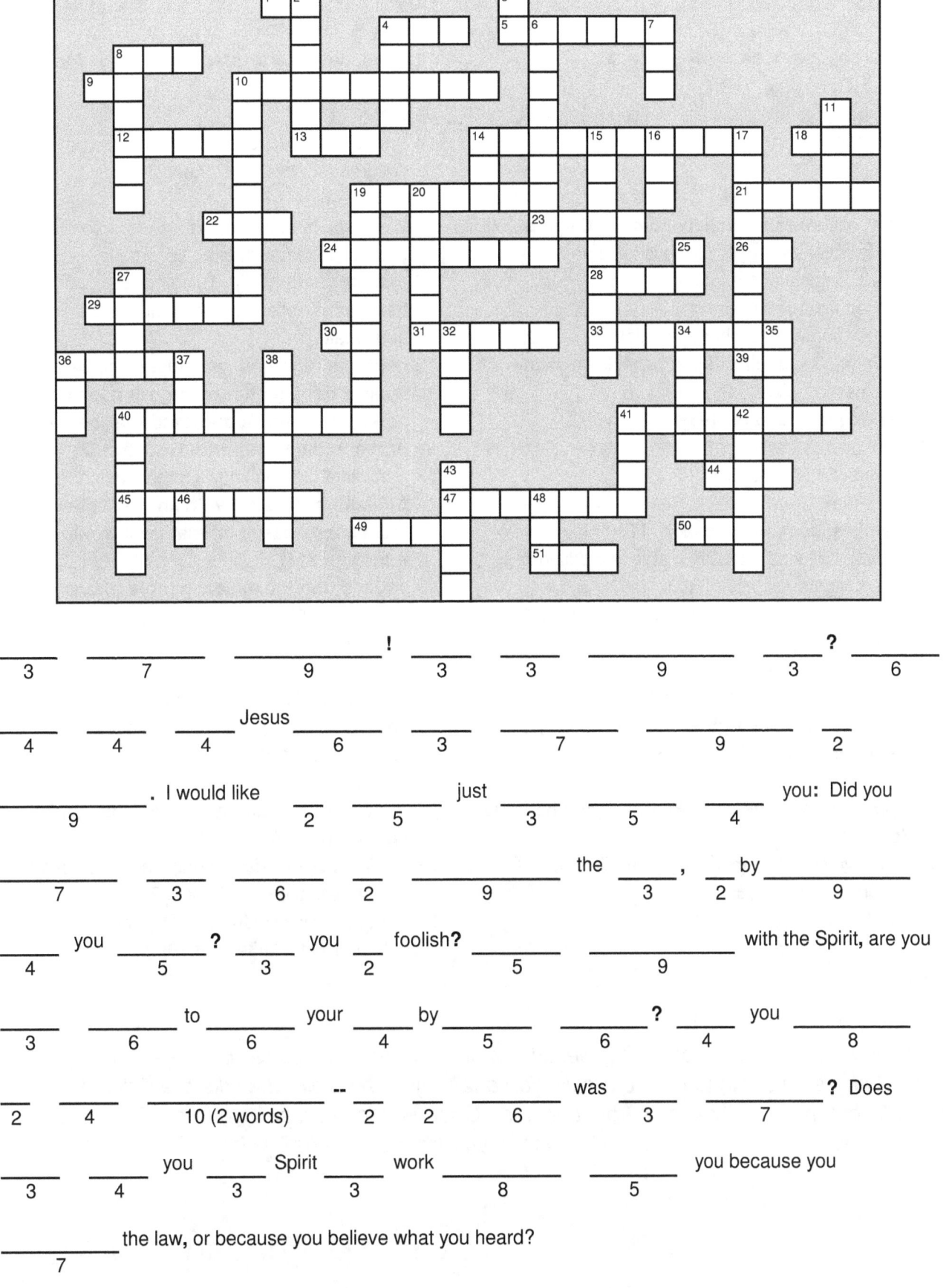

___ ___ ___ ___ ! ___ ___ ___ ___ ? ___
3   7   9   3   3   9   3   6

___ ___ ___ Jesus ___ ___ ___ ___ ___
4   4   4   6   3   7   9   2

_____. I would like ___ ___ just ___ ___ ___ you: Did you
     9   2   5   3   5   4

___ ___ ___ ___ ___ the ___ , ___ by ___
7   3   6   2   9   3   2   9

___ you ___ ? ___ you ___ foolish? ___ _____ with the Spirit, are you
4   5   3   5   9

___ ___ to ___ your ___ by ___ ___ ? ___ you ___
3   6   6   4   5   6   4   8

___ ___ _____ -- ___ ___ ___ was ___ ___ ? Does
2   4   10 (2 words)   2   2   6   3   7

___ ___ you ___ Spirit ___ work ___ ___ you because you
3   4   3   3   8   5

_____ the law, or because you believe what you heard?
    7

41

Galatians 3:6-9

ACROSS

2 "...all peoples on earth will be blessed _____ you." (Gen. 12:3)
6 "...those ___ have faith are blessed along with Abraham…" (3:9)
7 early
11 every
12 **holy, authoritative collection of writings (p. 82)**
15 "...My covenant __ your flesh is to be an everlasting covenant." (Gen. 17:13)
16 consequently, therefore
17 association with another (2 words)
18 "...Through your offspring all peoples on earth will __ blessed." (Acts 3:25)
19 **the one true God (p. 193)**
20 also, even, likewise
21 therefore, consequently
23 that man
24 **Gentiles, pagans, people (p. 116)**
25 "Abram believed the LORD, and he credited it __ him as righteousness." (Gen. 15:6)
27 "...I ____ made you a father of many nations." (Rom. 4:17)
28 "...Abraham believed God, and it ___ credited to him as righteousness." (Rom. 4:3)
30 **vindicate, declare righteous and in a proper relationship with God (p. 102)**
32 **know, recognize (p. 80)**
34 **spoken well of, be given kindness and benefits (p. 140)**
35 "...I have chosen him, so ____ he will direct his children…" (Gen. 18:19)

DOWN

1 **sons, daughters, offspring, descendants (p. 404)**
3 that man
4 "...out __ these stones God can raise up children for Abraham." (Luke 3:8)
5 good news
7 "...when a man works, his wages ___ not credited to him as a gift…" (Rom. 4:4)
8 *"father of many"* **(p. 1)**, father of Isaac
9 think about, reflect on, contemplate
10 adult male
13 **counted; regarded, considered (p. 249)**
14 **what is right, justice, doing what is in agreement with God's standards, being in proper relationship with God (p. 102)**
17 proclaimed, made known, broadcasted
18 **put faith in, trusted, with an implication that actions based on that trust would follow (p. 314)**
19 **pagans; foreign nation, people who are not Jews (p. 116)**
22 "...We have Abraham __ our father…" (Luke 3:8)
26 "...God promised him that he and his descendants after him _____ possess the land…" (Acts 7:5)
29 the thing
31 **trust, the Christian system of belief and lifestyle (p. 314)**
33 "I will make your descendants as numerous as ___ stars in the sky…" (Gen. 26:4)
34 "...keep the way of the LORD __ doing what is right and just…" (Gen. 18:19)

Even after being saved by faith in Jesus Christ under the new convenant, we sometimes forget and start trying to earn our salvation again by works. Good works are definitely good…but they don't save us from our sins. Good works are a service to our Lord and Savior Jesus Christ. What is God saying to you from Galatians? --Jan

Galatians 3:6-9

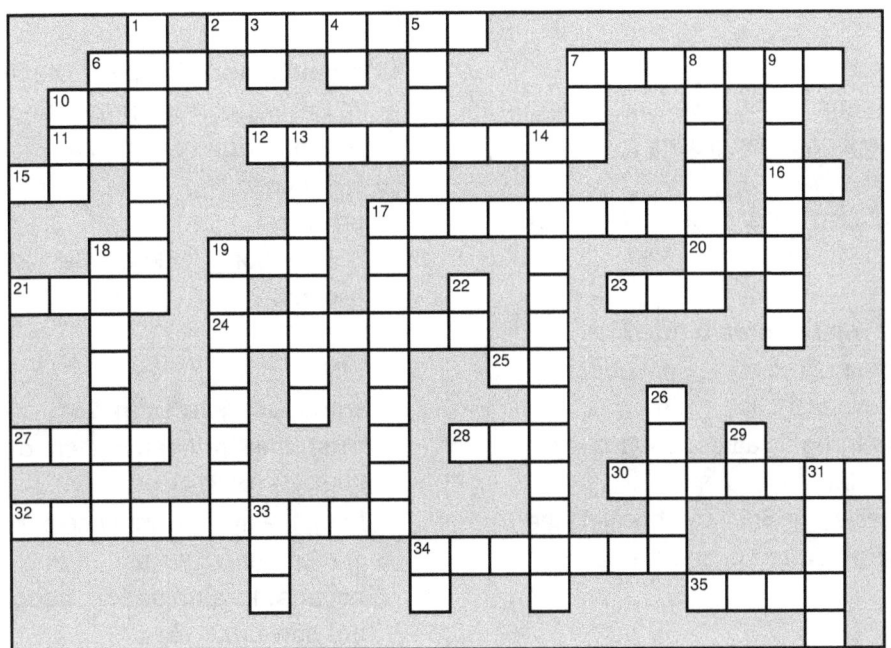

___ ___ : " ___ ___ , ___ ___ ___ ___
 8   7   2   8   3   3   2   3   8

___ ___ ___ ." ___ , ___ , ___ those ___
 2   3   2   13   10   4   4   3

believe ___ ___ ___ Abraham. ___ ___ foresaw that God
         3   8   2   3   9

___ ___ the ___ ___ ___ , and ___ the ___
 5   7   8   2   5   9   6

___ ___ to Abraham: " ___ ___ will ___ ___ ___
 2   7   3   7   2   7   7

you." ___ those who ___ faith are blessed ___ Abraham, the ___ of faith.
       2   4   9 (2 words)   3

43

Galatians 3:10-14

ACROSS

1 in no way
3 "Listen to the terms __ this covenant…" (Jer. 11:2)
5 **praise, thanksgiving, generosity (p. 174)**
10 you and I
11 "…a man is not justified by observing ___ law…" (2:16)
12 in the sight of
14 **God the Holy wind or breath (p. 331)**
16 "…Cursed is the man who ____ not obey the terms of this covenant" (Jer. 11:3)
17 "…are you now trying __ attain your goal by human effort?" (3:3)
18 "…Did you receive ___ Spirit by observing the law, or by believing what you heard?" (3:2)
19 the thing
20 every person
21 the thing
22 could, may
24 adult male
25 exist, survive
26 **Anointed One, Messiah, Son of David, Jesus who came to bring liberty from sin and peace with God and who will come again to bring all things under his control (p. 439)**
27 **vindicated, declared righteous, in a proper relationship with God (p. 102)**
28 are determined to or resolved to
30 **a person in accord with God's standards, in proper relationship with God (p. 102)**
34 "Cursed __ the man who does not uphold the words of this law…" (Deut. 27:26)
35 "…a man is not justified by observing the law, but by faith __ Jesus Christ…" (2:16)
36 out of
37 nuisance, irritation, annoyance
38 you and me
39 but, instead, yet, except (3 words)
41 **the one true God (p. 193)**
43 "For if those who live by law ___ heirs, faith has no value…" (Rom. 4:14)
44 **scroll (p. 70); manuscript**
46 each person
47 trust in, put your faith in, depend on (2 words)
48 **regulations, principles; the first five books of the Scriptures, or any single command of the Scriptures (p. 279)**
50 suspended
51 practice
52 "…Is he not ___ God of Gentiles too? Yes…" (Rom. 3:29)

DOWN

2 **wood, post, cross (p. 281)**
4 **trust, the Christian system of belief and lifestyle (p. 314)**
5 from; the means or source of (2 words)
6 in order that (2 words)
7 **pagans; foreign nation, people who are not Jews (p. 116)**
8 **set free, reclaimed (p. 143)**
9 **working (p. 165);** abiding by, respecting, following, complying with
10 in a form to be read
13 "__ if the inheritance depends on the law, then it no longer depends on a promise…" (3:18)
15 assurance, guarantee, agreement
20 *"father of many"* **(p. 1),** father of Isaac
23 deeds done
26 plainly, evidently
27 **Joshua, "*Yahweh saves*" (p. 200)**
29 "…where there __ no law there is no transgression." (Rom. 4:15)
30 take
31 "…man is justified by faith apart from observing ___ law." (Rom. 3:28)
32 for the purpose that, so that (3 words)
33 **remain faithful (p. 135);** carry on
38 beneath
40 called evil, afflicted
41 presented
42 not anyone (2 words)
44 "…the righteous will live __ his faith" (Hab. 2:4)
45 "…anyone who is hung __ a tree is under God's curse…" (Deut. 21:23)
49 "You foolish Galatians! ___ has bewitched you?" (3:1)

Galatians 3:10-14

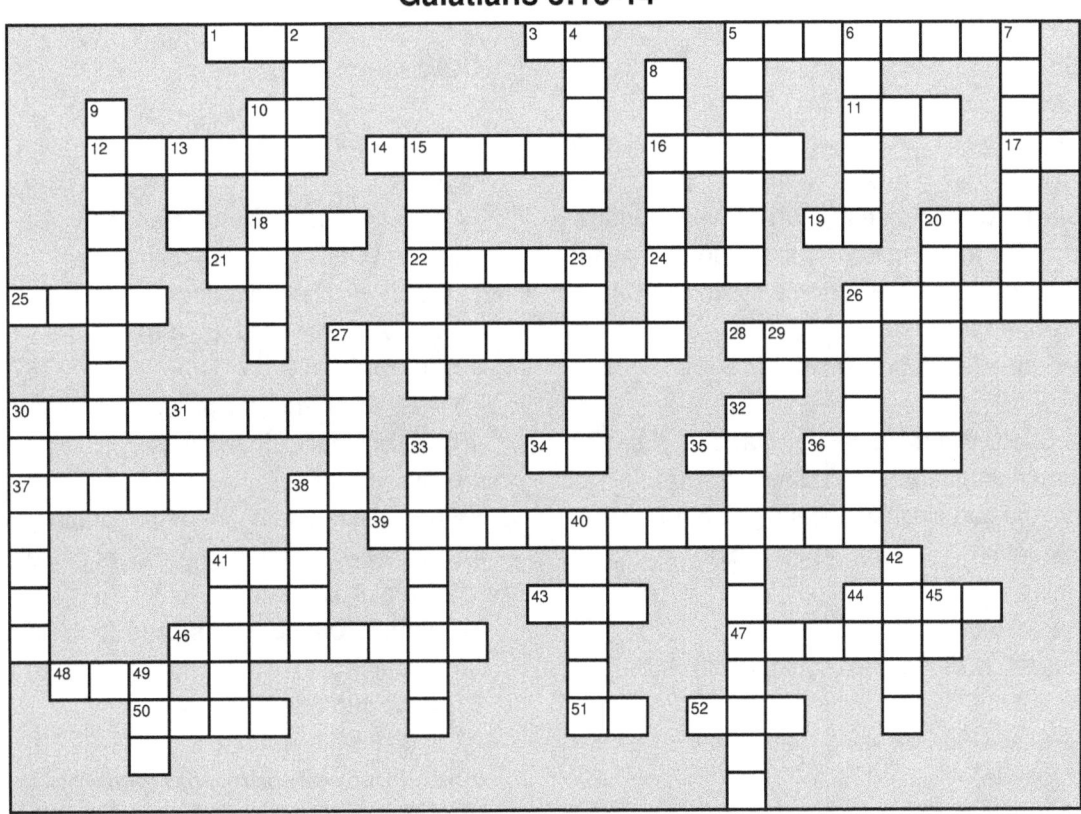

___ ___ _____ (2 words) ___ ___ ___ ___ ___a
 3   3   6   9   3   3   3   5

_____, ___ __ __ _____ :" _____ __ _____ who ____
   5   3   2   2   7   6   2   8   4

___ _____ everything written ___ ___ ____ __ ___ law."
 3   8   2   3   4   2   3

_____ is _____ ___ ___ ___ ___ law, because,
   7   5 (2 words) 9   6   3   2   3

"The _____ ____ by _____." The law is not _____ faith;
        9   4   5   7 (2 words)

_____, "The ___ who does these _____ will live by them."
 13 (3 words)   3   6   6

_____ __ ____ the curse of the law by becoming a curse for us, for __ is written: "Cursed
   8   2   4   2

is everyone who is ____ a ____." He redeemed us _____ the
                    4   4   11 (3 words)

_____ _____ to _____ _____ come to the _____ through Christ
   8   5   7   5   8

_____, _____ by faith might ___ _____ the _____ of the _____.
  5   6 (2 words)   2   7   6

45

Galatians 3:15-18

ACROSS

1 "...you will tread our sins underfoot and hurl all our iniquities into ___ depths of the sea." (Mic. 7:19)
4 **Anointed One, Messiah, Son of David, Jesus who came to bring liberty from sin and peace with God and who will come again to bring all things under his control (p. 439)**
6 provided, offered, presented
8 also
9 "The LORD swore an oath __ David..." (Ps. 132:11)
10 assurances, guarantees, oaths
12 "When he had finished speaking with Abraham, God went up ____ him." (Gen. 17:22)
13 the thing
14 human being, individual
17 hinges on, is determined by (2 words)
19 allow, permit
22 general term for speaking
24 through, via
25 therefore, consequently, as a result
26 have in mind
27 belonging to you
28 "Who __ a God like you, who pardons sin..." (Mic. 7:18)
30 consequently
31 on the contrary
32 "He ___ shown you, O man, what is good..." (Mic. 6:8)
33 Bible text
35 "...he built an altar there to the LORD, ___ had appeared to him." (Gen. 12:7)
37 "What ____ the Scripture say?..." (Rom. 4:3)
40 the thing
41 **ratified beforehand (p. 345) (2 words)**
43 in no way
44 **nullify, abolish, make ineffective (p. 219) (3 words)**
46 not anybody (2 words)
48 existence of human beings
51 increase (2 words)
52 **forgiveness, cancellation of debt (p. 433)**
55 "You, my brothers, ____ called to be free..." (5:13)
56 coming into existence; presented

DOWN

2 illustration
3 daily
4 situation, set of circumstances
5 "The LORD swore an oath to David, a sure oath ____ he will not revoke..." (Ps. 132:11)
6 **the one true God (p. 193)**
7 on condition that
8 *"father of many"* **(p. 1), father of Isaac**
10 persons, folks, individuals
11 myself, I
15 not again, not any more, no further (2 words)
16 "...He is our father __ the sight of God..." (Rom. 4:17)
18 **hidden, concealed, stored (p. 242) (2 words)**
20 the thing
21 at the same time (2 words)
23 sets of twelve months
29 **children, offspring, descendants (p. 372)**
30 **reject (p. 8) (2 words)**
31 **fellow countrymen, neighbors; fellow believers in the family of faith; regularly refers to men and women (p. 6)**
34 **solemn agreement; will, testament (p. 96)**
36 belonging to him
38 said, told
39 "This __ my covenant with you and your descendants after you..." (Gen. 17:10)
42 **a share, participation in privileges (p. 233) (2 words)**
45 "...God had power to do ____ he had promised." (Rom. 4:21)
47 individual
48 **regulation, principle; first five books of the Scriptures, or any single command of the Scriptures (p. 279)**
49 "...As ___ you, you must keep my covenant, you and your descendants after you..." (Gen. 17:9)
50 alternately
51 "...I will establish my covenant with him as __ everlasting covenant..." (Gen. 17:19)
53 is able to
54 also

Galatians 3:15-18

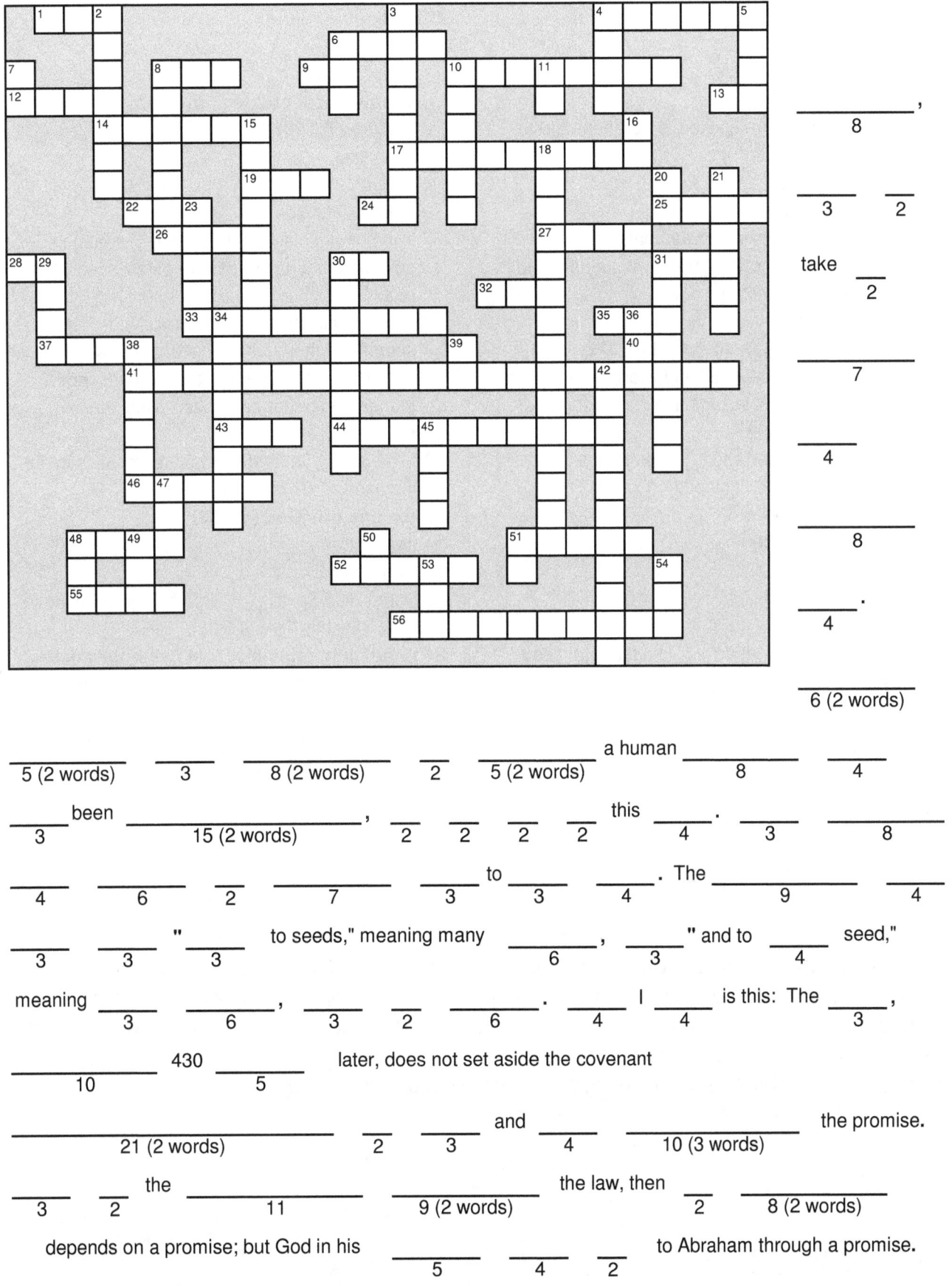

Galatians 3:19-20

ACROSS

1 symbolize, characterize
4 however
5 "___ promises were spoken to Abraham and to his seed..." (Gal. 3:16)
6 participant, group
11 **violations (p. 300)**
13 assurance, guarantee, agreement, oath
15 "A faithful God who ____ no wrong, upright and just is he." (Deut. 32:4)
16 brought, given
18 **Child, Offspring, Descendant (p. 372)**
20 "For if there ___ been nothing wrong with that first covenant, no place would have been sought for another." (Heb. 8:7)
21 "...through the obedience __ the one man the many will be made righteous." (Rom. 5:19)
22 on the other hand
23 **messengers (p. 3)**
25 the thing
26 arrived, appeared
27 only, merely
29 "...God had power to do ____ he had promised." (Rom. 4:21)

DOWN

1 talked about
2 **commanded, ordered, directed; to be required (p. 96) (3 words)**
3 in no way
4 through
6 reason, intention
7 "...no one can set aside or add __ a human covenant that has been duly established..." (Gal. 3:15)
8 "But the ministry Jesus has received __ as superior to theirs as the covenant of which he is mediator is superior to the old one, and it is founded on better promises." (Heb. 8:6)
9 single
10 "The law ___ added so that the trespass might increase..." (Rom. 5:20)
12 **the one true God (p. 193)**
14 negotiator
17 by means of
19 "...the Holy Spirit, ____ God has given to those who obey him." (Acts 5:32)
24 **regulation, principle; first five books of the Scriptures, or any single command of the Scriptures (p. 279)**
28 "...where sin increased, grace increased all ___ more," (Rom. 5:20)

We can't be saved by both our works and by faith in Jesus Christ. It's only by faith in Jesus. We can't be saved by our works because we are also sinners, and therefore undeserving. The law was provided to teach us right from wrong...to teach us what is best versus what is damaging and hurtful. So, the law is still important, but keeping the law does not save. What is God saying to you from Galatians? --Jan

Galatians 3:19-20

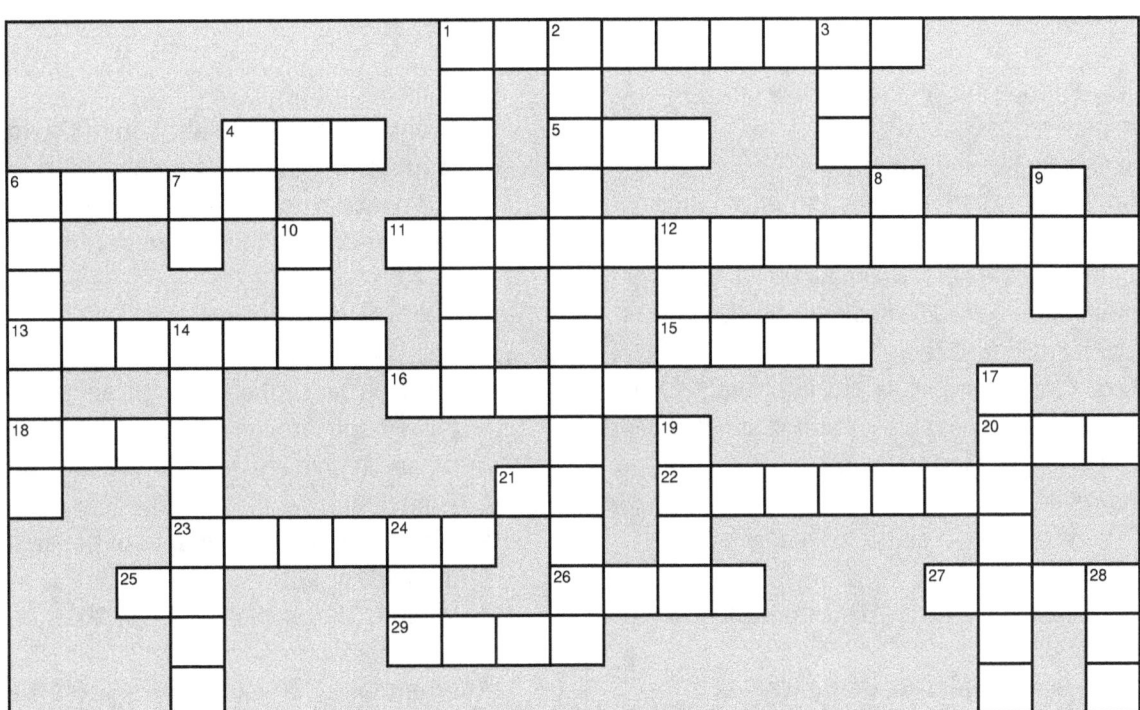

____ , then, ____ ____ ____ ____ ____ ____ ?
  4   3   3   7   2   3   3   2

was ____ because of ____ until the ____ ____ ____
     5   14   4   2   4

the ____ ____ ____ ____ . The law was
     7   8   3   4

____ ____ ____ ____ a
13 (3 words)   7   6   2

____ . A mediator, ____ , ____ ____ ____
 8   7   4   3   9

____ ____ ____ ; ____ ____ ____ one.
 4   3   5   3   3   2

Galatians 3:21-22

ACROSS

1 "For through the law I died to the law ___ that I might live for God." (2:19)
3 is able to, has the power to
5 **holy, authoritative collection of writings (p. 82)**
7 existed, been presented
9 "...For I would not have known what coveting really was ___ the law had not said, 'Do not covet.'" (Rom. 7:7)
11 "For if those who live by law are heirs, faith has no value and the promise ___ worthless," (Rom. 4:14)
12 **the one true God (p. 193)**
13 however
14 "Therefore, ___ promise comes by faith…" (Rom. 4:16)
16 "...there is not one ___ does good, not even one." (Rom. 3:12)
17 **what is right, justice, doing what is in agreement with God's standards, being in proper relationship with God (p. 102)**
19 "For everything that ___ written in the past was written to teach us…" (Rom. 15:4)
20 not at all, not a bit (2 words)
22 out of; from
25 **make alive, give life to (p. 183) (2 words)**
27 consequently
29 assurances, guarantees, oaths
30 presented, provided
32 entire
34 "I have ____ crucified with Christ and I no longer live, but Christ lives in me…" (Gal. 2:20)
35 "know that a man is not justified by observing the law, but by faith ___ Jesus Christ…" (2:16)
36 "...Indeed I _____ not have known what sin was except through the law." (Rom. 7:7)

DOWN

2 against, contrary to (2 words)
3 **Anointed One, Messiah, Son of David, Jesus who came to bring liberty from sin and peace with God and who will come again to bring all things under his control (p. 439)**
4 says, announces, proclaims
6 really, surely
8 "...just as sin reigned in death, so also grace _____ reign through righteousness to bring eternal life through Jesus Christ our Lord." (Rom. 5:21)
10 **trust, the Christian system of belief and lifestyle (p. 314)**
15 **Joshua, "*Yahweh saves*" (p. 200)**
16 earth; human race
18 **wrongdoing; any act contrary to the will and law of God (p. 17)**
19 "...For I have the desire to do ____ is good, but I cannot carry it out." (Rom. 7:18)
21 out of, by way of
22 **put one's faith in, trust, with an implication that actions based on that trust may follow (p. 314)**
23 "It was not through law that Abraham and his offspring received the promise that he would be heir ___ the world, but through the righteousness that comes by faith." (Rom. 4:13)
24 guaranteed
26 **someone enclosed, shut up (p. 380)**
27 "For God has bound all men over ___ disobedience so that he may have mercy on them all." (Rom. 11:32)
28 "...___ if righteousness could be gained through the law, Christ died for nothing!" (2:21)
31 "Understand, ____, that those who believe are children of Abraham." (3:7)
33 **regulation, principle; first five books of the Scriptures, or any single command of the Scriptures (p. 279)**
34 "...we seek to ___ justified in Christ…" (2:17)

Galatians 3:21-22

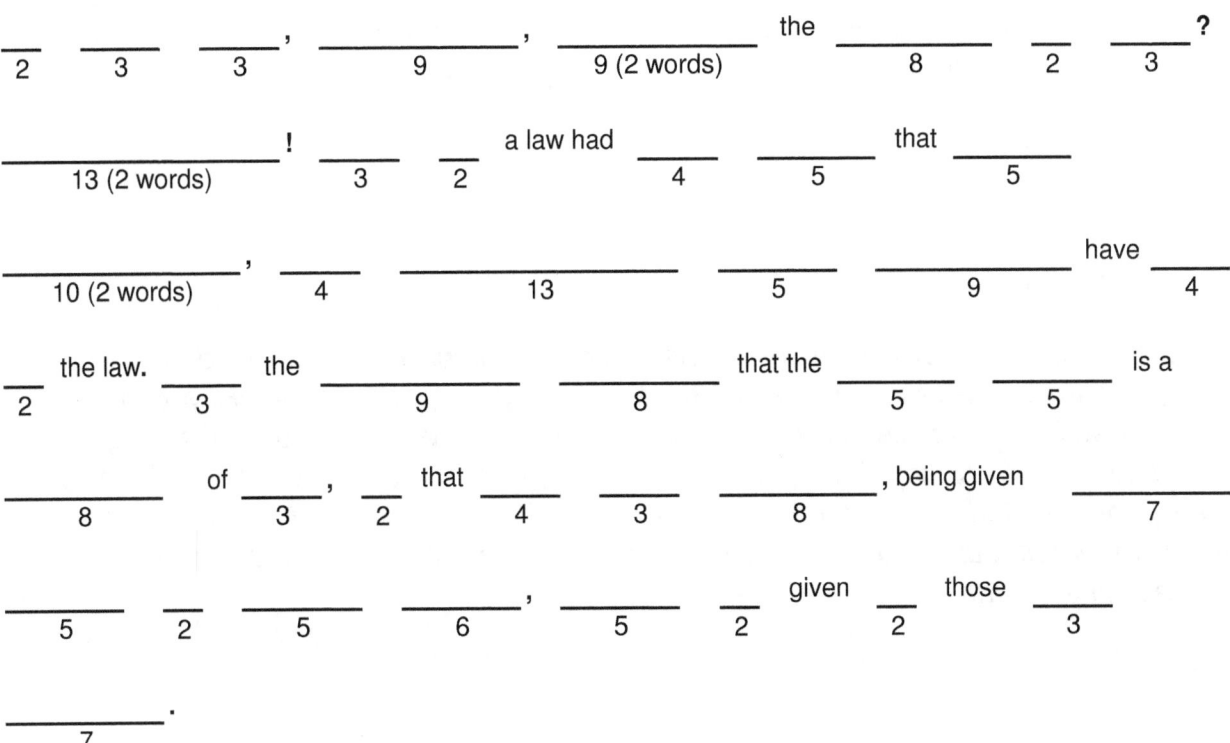

Galatians 3:23-25

ACROSS

2 arrived, appeared, got here
3 **Anointed One, Messiah, Son of David, Jesus who came to bring liberty from sin and peace with God and who will come again to bring all things under his control (p. 439)**
7 **vindicated, declared righteous, in a proper relationship with God (p. 102)**
8 beneath, below
10 **guarding, supervising, made custodian (p. 298)** (5 words)
15 **guardianship, custody (p. 298)**
16 "...a righteousness from God, apart from law, ___ been made known..." (Rom. 3:21)
17 "Oh, the depth __ the riches of the wisdom and knowledge of God!" (Rom. 11:33)
18 awaiting, in anticipation of
19 "Just as you who ____ at one time disobedient to God..." (Rom. 11:30)
20 "...Jews and Gentiles alike ___ all under sin." (Rom. 3:9)
21 **caught, confined, imprisoned (p. 380) (2 words)**
22 "It ___ not through law that Abraham and his offspring received the promise..." (Rom. 4:13)

DOWN

1 you and me
2 arrived, appeared, got here
4 **kept, guarded, shielded (p. 430) (2 words)**
5 **trust, the Christian system of belief and lifestyle (p. 314)**
6 "...so that every mouth may __ silenced and the whole world held accountable to God." (Rom. 3:19)
9 not again, not any more, no further (2 words)
11 "...the promise comes by faith, so that it may be by grace and may be guaranteed __ all Abraham's offspring..." (Rom. 4:16)
12 **disclosed, announced (p. 42)**
13 "____ is why 'it was credited to him as righteousness.'" (Rom. 4:22)
14 "...We have already made ___ charge that Jews and Gentiles alike are all under sin." (Rom. 3:9)
15 for this reason, therefore
19 you and I
21 **regulation, principle; first five books of the Scriptures, or any single command of the Scriptures (p. 279)**

Why do we make it so hard when Jesus has made it so simple? Is it our pride that causes us to try to earn our salvation by keeping the law and by our good works? How can we try to compete with the sacrifice of the God who created the universe...who is all seeing...all knowing...who is everything?! Why do we try to compete? Why can't we simply humble ourselves before God and accept His beautiful gift? There are so many things that we try to make important, but nothing is more important than that! What is God saying to you from Galatians? --Jan

Galatians 3:23-25

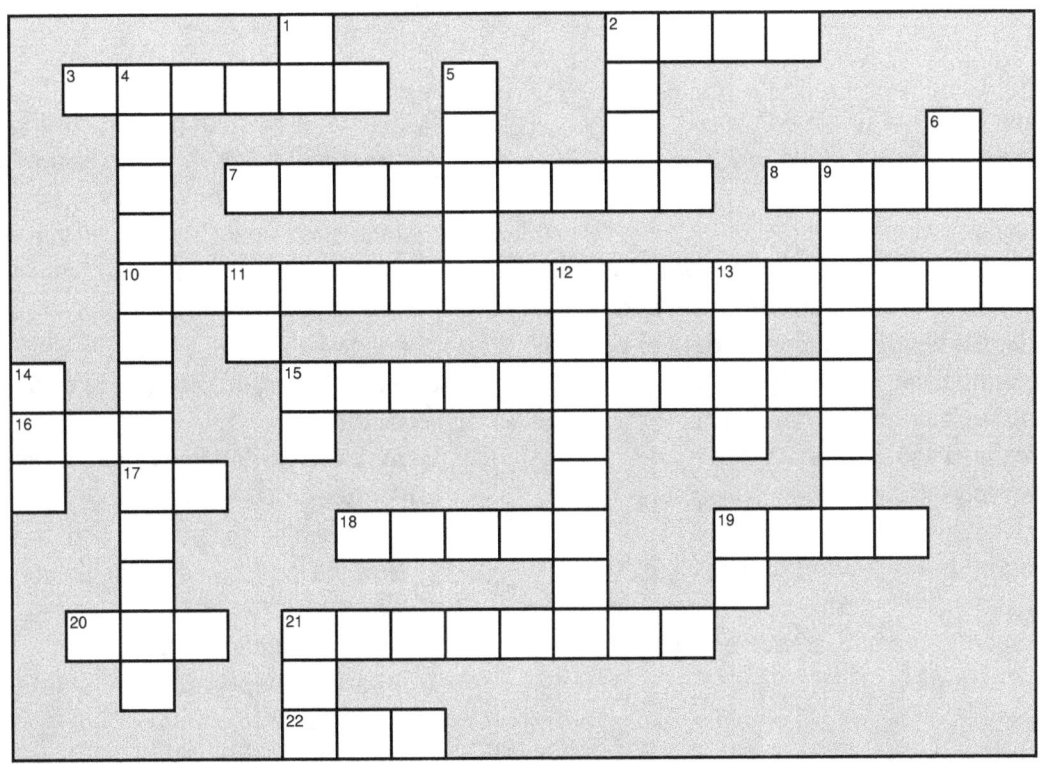

Before _____ _____ _____ , _____ _____
          4   5   4   2   13 (2 words)

by _____ _____ , _____ _____ faith should
      3   3   8 (2 words)   5   2

_____ . _____ the law _____ _____
   8   2   17 (5 words)   2

__ _____ that we might be _____ by faith. Now that faith _____
 2   6   9   3

_____ , we _____ _____ _____ the _____
    4   3   8 (2 words)   5   11

_____ the law.
    2

53

Galatians 3:26-29

ACROSS

1 single
3 **the one true God (p. 193)**
4 **opposite of being a slave (p. 131)**
6 not either
9 pertaining to women
12 **Anointed One, Messiah, Son of David, Jesus who came to bring liberty from sin and peace with God and who will come again to bring all things under his control (p. 439)**
13 "...teaching them to obey everything I ____ commanded you..." (Matt. 28:20)
14 "...you received the Spirit __ sonship..." (Rom. 8:15)
15 **belonging to the "*father of many*" (p. 1)**
19 also
20 assurance, guarantee, agreement, oath
22 toward and within
23 everyone
24 dressed
26 descendant of Jacob
28 "The promises were spoken __ Abraham and to his seed..." (3:16)
29 all of you personally
30 "...baptizing them __ the name of the Father and of the Son and of the Holy Spirit," (Matt. 28:19)
31 **children (of either gender), descendants (in any generation) (p. 413)**

DOWN

2 and not
3 **Gentile, a class of person distinguished from the Jewish race and nation (p. 133)**
4 "___ you did not receive a spirit that makes you a slave again to fear..." (Rom. 8:15)
5 "...those who ___ led by the Spirit of God are sons of God. (Rom. 8:14)
7 those who inherit
8 **servant; person pledged or bound to serve (p. 106)**
9 **trust, the Christian system of belief and lifestyle (p. 314)**
10 in, by, with, in accordance with, for (2 words)
11 "Now the body __ not made up of one part but of many." (1 Cor. 12:14)
16 **washed, immersed (p. 65)**
17 **children, offspring, descendants (p. 372)**
18 by means of
21 pertaining to men
25 "Here _____ is no Greek or Jew, circumcised or uncircumcised..." (Col. 3:11)
26 **Joshua, "*Yahweh saves*" (p. 200)**
27 "...all of us ___ were baptized into Christ Jesus were baptized into his death" (Rom. 6:3)
28 consequently
29 "...if by the Spirit ___ put to death the misdeeds of the body, you will live" (Rom. 8:13)
30 "...there __ not one who does good, not even one." (Rom. 3:12)

In Jesus Christ, we believers are all children of God. Do you think of yourself as a child of God? Jews, Gentiles, and people of all shapes, sizes, and colors...we can all be children of God when we believe in that love and salvation. What is God saying to you from Galatians? --Jan

Galatians 3:26-29

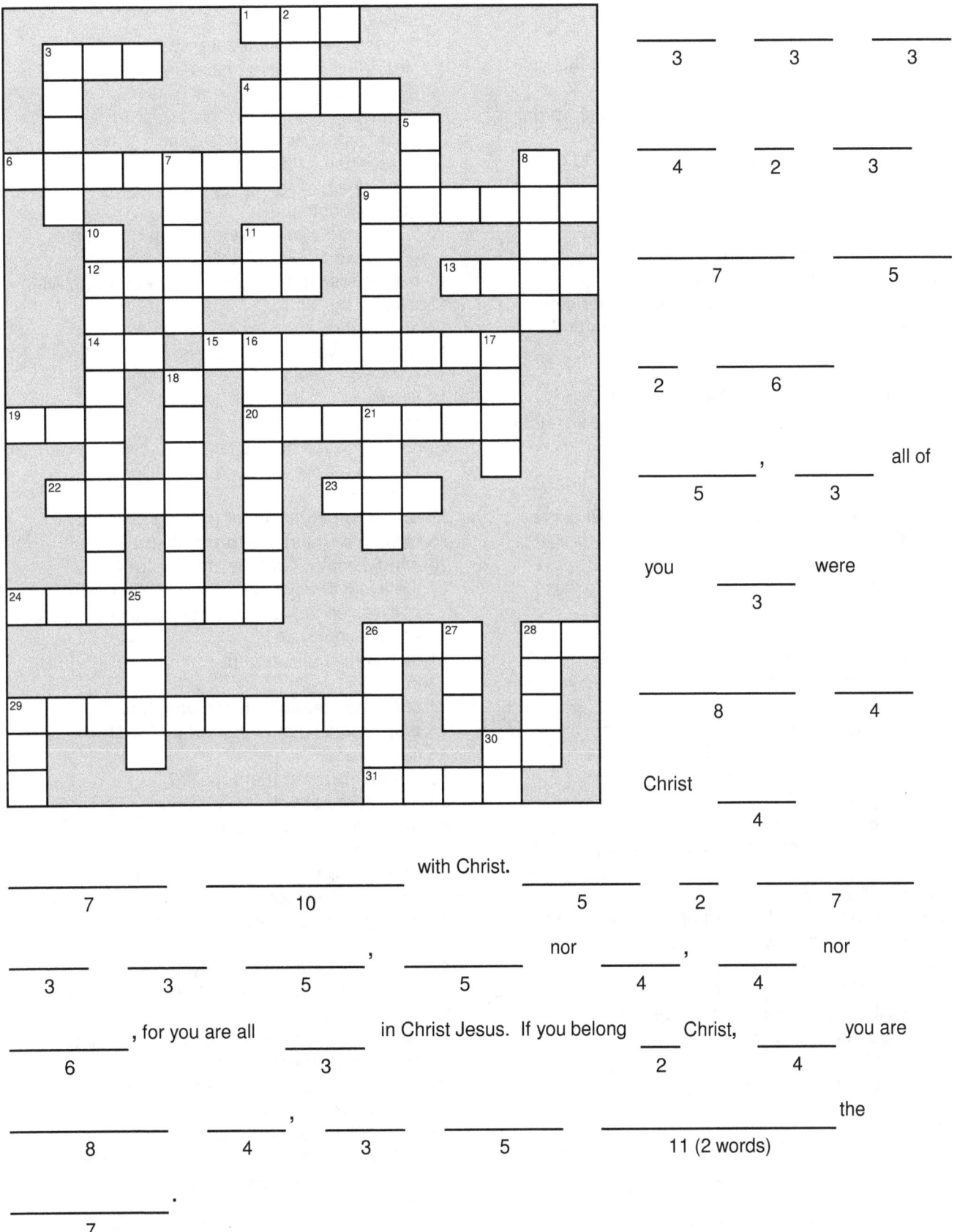

Galatians 4:1-7

ACROSS

1 "But now ____ you know God..." (4:9)
3 that man
4 "...so that the truth __ the gospel might remain with you." (2:5)
7 **cries out, shouts, exclaims (p. 239)** (2 words)
12 beneath authority
14 **infant; implication of immaturity (p. 277)**
15 **Aramaic for "father" (p. 1)**
17 great period of time
18 "...a righteousness from God, apart from law, ___ been made known..." (Rom. 3:21)
19 **appointment (p. 344)** (2 words)
22 **minds, thoughts and emotions; inner selves (life, soul, mind, and spirit), thinking and understanding (p. 213)**
24 likewise
28 **elementary rules (p. 376)** (2 words)
30 "...Hagar...is __ slavery with her children." (4:25)
31 privileges, claims
32 came, delivered
33 because
34 **servant; person pledged or bound to serve (p. 106)**
35 **the one true God (p. 193)**
36 "...how __ it that you are turning back to those weak and miserable principles?..." (4:9)
37 not any
38 period between two events
40 "___ see, at just the right time, when we were still powerless, Christ died for the ungodly." (Rom. 5:6)
42 land, assets, property, fortune, wealth
45 **more valuable than (p. 97)** (2 words)
49 "...you ____ slaves to those who by nature are not gods." (4:8)
51 toward and within
53 "Therefore, brothers, we have __ obligation..." (Rom. 8:12)
54 also, likewise
55 "...false brothers had infiltrated our ranks to spy on ___ freedom we have in Christ..." (2:4)
56 one who inherits
57 general term for speaking
58 **earth system, whole universe; a system opposed to God (p. 238)**
60 female
61 after, as soon as

DOWN

2 belonging to him
3 "...because in his forbearance he ___ left the sins committed beforehand unpunished" (Rom. 3:25)
5 complete
6 "...the redemption of those who ___ God's possession..." (Eph. 1:14)
8 "...I __ perplexed about you! (4:20)
9 greater length
10 "...you died with Christ to the basic principles __ this world..." (Col. 2:20)
11 **managers, administrators, directors (p. 284)**
13 even if
14 approached
15 "...just __ you received Christ Jesus as Lord, continue to live in him..." (Col. 2:6)
16 since
20 therefore
21 "See __ it that no one takes you captive through hollow and deceptive philosophy..." (Col. 2:8)
23 **under the authority of (p. 417)** (2 words)
25 **is Lord or master of property (p. 244)**
26 **wind, breath, God the Holy Spirit (p. 331)**
27 the event of a person owning another as a possession for various lengths of times
29 infants, immature
31 be given, obtain, accept
32 through
33 **child, descendant; messianic title, emphasizes Jesus' humanity (p. 413)**
34 therefore
35 **overseers, managers (p. 162)**
39 named, produced
41 rather; on the other hand
43 delivered
44 also, likewise
46 completely, entirely, totally
47 **male parent or ancestor (p. 312)**
48 may
49 "____ has happened to all your joy?..." (4:15)
50 **set free, rescue, buy (p. 143)**
52 yours and mine
57 **children (of either gender), descendants (in any generation) (p. 413)**
58 "that everyone ___ believes in him may have eternal life." (John 3:15)
59 **regulations, principles; the first five books of the Scriptures, or any single command of the Scriptures (p. 279)**
60 you and I

Galatians 4:1-7

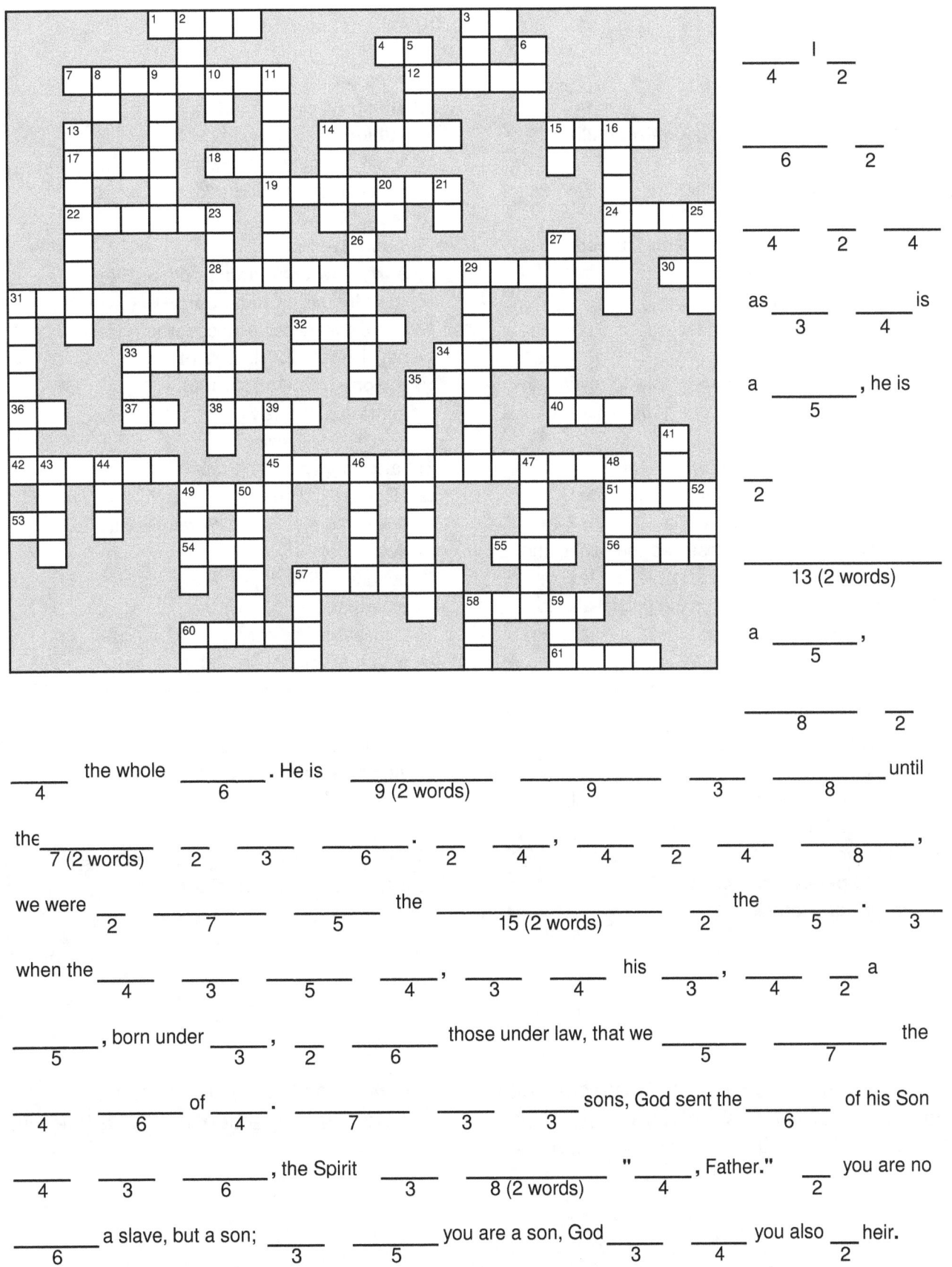

57

Galatians 4:8-11

ACROSS

1. at the present time
2. on behalf of
5. **possess information; recognize, realize; understand (p. 283)**
6. character, personality, makeup
8. Before
10. "...think of what you ___ when you were called..." (1 Cor. 1:26)
11. **servants (p. 107)**
13. the thing
14. instead
15. "...they ___ not think it worthwhile to retain the knowledge of God..." (Rom. 1:28)
16. true divine spirits
19. **elementary rules (p. 376)**
20. "For we are God's workmanship, created in Christ Jesus to __ good works..." (Eph. 2:10)
21. "Come back __ your senses as you ought, and stop sinning..." (1 Cor. 15:34)
23. "...I am so eager to preach the gospel also to ___..." (Rom. 1:15)
25. once more (3 words)
28. "For God did not call us to __ impure..." (1 Thes. 4:7)
29. 24-hour periods of time
32. through
33. "...God was pleased...to save those ___ believe." (1 Cor. 1:21)
34. at the time
36. **limited periods of time (p. 209)**
37. **imperfect, inefficient (p. 55)**

DOWN

1. in no way
2. **am afraid or alarmed (p. 428)**
3. **subjected to service (p. 107)**
4. "I will pronounce my judgments __ my people because of their wickedness in forsaking me..." (Jer. 1:16)
7. works, labors
9. **sorry, low condition, poor (p. 356)**
10. **tried in vain or to no purpose (p. 117)**
12. "...evil that deceives those who ___ perishing..." (2 Thes. 2:10)
16. **the one true God (p. 193)**
17. particular, exclusive
18. also, even, likewise
21. **returning (p. 161) (2 words)**
22. "They ___ thrown their gods into the fire and destroyed them, for they were not gods..." (Isa. 37:19)
23. periods of 365 days
24. otherwise
25. also, even, likewise
26. **watching closely (p. 306)**
27. "So you ___ no longer a slave, but a son..." (4:7)
30. in what way
31. **viewed with favor (p. 80)**; recognized, understood
33. want, desire
35. "For it __ by grace you have been saved, through faith..." (Eph. 2:8)

Not only can we be God's children, but God's children are also God's heirs. Let's not go backwards...back to the slavery of trying to earn it all when we can accept it all as a free gift. What is God saying to you from Galatians? --Jan

Galatians 4:8-11

____ , ____ ____ ____ ____ ____ ____ , you ____ ____ ____
 8   4   3   3   3   4   3   4   6   2

those ____ ____ ____ ____ not ____ . But ____ that you know God-- ____
       3   2   6   3   4   3   2

____ ____ ____ by God-- ____ ____ ____ that you are _____ to those
 6   3   5   3   2   2   11 (2 words)

____ ____ ____ ____ ? ____ you ____ to ____
 4   3   9   10   2   4   2   8

by them _____ ? You are ____ ____ ____ ____
        12 (3 words)   9   7   4   3

months and ____ and ____ ! I ____ you, that somehow I ____
            7   5   4   3   4

____ my ____ ____ you.
 6   7   2

59

Galatians 4:12-16

ACROSS

1 fact, reality, honesty
3 also, likewise
7 look upon, behave toward
8 ridiculing, rejection, despising
11 **messenger; supernatural being that serves God (p. 3)**
13 "For when we ____ controlled by the sinful nature...we bore fruit for death." (Rom. 7:5)
14 speaking to
18 **it had been possible for you, you had been able (p. 108)** (5 words)
22 in no way
24 before, formerly, an earlier time
25 **received kindly (p. 88)**
28 belonging to me
29 **dug through, pluck out (p. 147)** (2 words)
32 **happiness (p. 256)**
33 possess information; recognize, realize; understand
37 **give evidence, declare (p. 258)**
39 organs of sight
41 **the one true God (p. 193)**
43 every part of
44 "My message and my preaching were...with a demonstration __ the Spirit's power." (1 Cor. 2:4)
45 "...to him who ___ raised from the dead..." (Rom. 7:4)
48 **neglect, disregard, contempt, rejection (p. 148)**
51 occurred, come to pass
52 at the present time

DOWN

1 those things
2 "...I am speaking to men who know ___ law..." (Rom. 7:1)
4 "...so that the body of sin might be ____ away with..." (Rom. 6:6)
5 **injury (p. 7)**
6 the thing
8 **Anointed One, Messiah, Son of David, Jesus who came to bring liberty from sin and peace with God and who will come again to bring all things under his control (p. 439)**

DOWN (continued)

9 **proclaimed the good news, which refers to Jesus' death, burial, and resurrection, as well as salvation through Jesus Christ (p. 172)** (3 words)
10 **test; temptation (p. 314)**
11 like
12 presented
15 "...though you ____ built stone mansions, you will not live in them..." (Amos 5:11)
16 through
17 "Therefore, __ we have opportunity, let us do good to all people..." (Gal. 6:10)
19 "...our Lord Jesus Christ, through which the world ___ been crucified to me..." (Gal. 6:14)
20 "...I ___ not come with eloquence or superior wisdom..." (1 Cor. 2:1)
21 opponent, adversary, foe, rival
23 **weakness, infirmity, sickness, suffering (p. 55)**
24 "...let no one cause me trouble, ___ I bear on my body the marks of Jesus." (6:17)
26 I, myself
27 "so ____ your faith might not rest on men's wisdom, but on God's power." (1 Cor. 2:5)
30 "Seek the Lord and live, __ he will sweep through the house of Joseph like a fire..." (Amos 5:6)
31 "You trample on the poor and force him __ give you grain..." (Amos 5:11)
32 **Joshua, "*Yahweh saves*" (p. 200)**
34 in the company of
35 on condition that
36 **pray; ask, beg (p. 89)**
38 belonging to you
40 "Do ___ not know, brothers...that the law has authority over a man only as long as he lives?" (Rom. 7:1)
42 "The grace __ our Lord Jesus Christ be with your spirit..." (6:18)
46 "This is ____ the LORD says to the house of Israel: 'Seek me and live'" (Amos 5:4)
47 "I laid a foundation as __ expert builder, and someone else is building on it..." (1 Cor. 3:10)
49 have the ability to
50 not any

Galatians 4:12-16

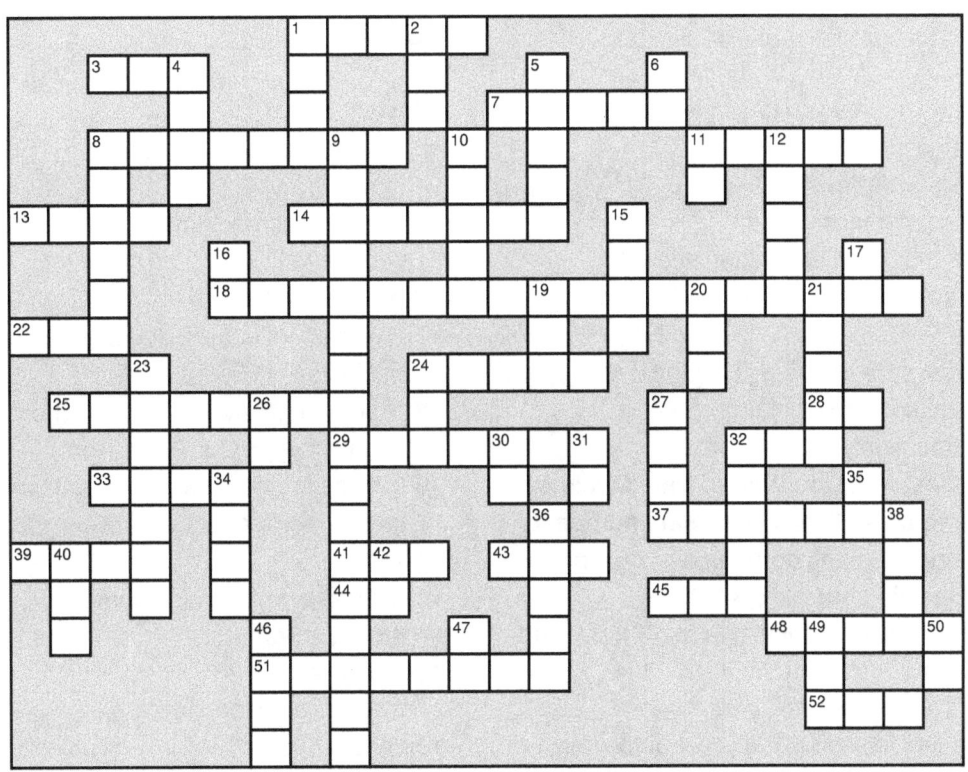

I ___ ___ ___, brothers, become like ___, ___ I became like you. You
      5   4   3   2   3   4

___ me ___. ___ you ___, ___ because ___ ___ ___
 4   2   5   2   4   2   3   2   2   7

___ I ___ _____ ___ you. Even though ___ illness was a
 4   5   17 (3 words)   2   2

___ to you, you ___ ___ ___ me with ___ ___ ___. Instead,
 5   3   3   5   8   2   5

you ___ me ___ I ___ an ___ ___, as if I were ___
     8   2   4   5   2   3   6

___ himself. ___ ___ ___ to ___ ___ ___ ? I
 5   4   3   8   3   4   3   3

___ that, if _____ you would have ___ your
 7   18 (5 words)   7 (2 words)   4

___ ___ ___ to me. Have I ___ become your ___ ___ ___
 3   5   4   3   5   2   7

you ___ ___ ?
     3   5

61

Galatians 4:17-20

ACROSS

1 "...___ is it, then, that you force Gentiles to follow Jewish customs?" (2:14)
3 **good, right; beautiful, excellent (p. 211)**
6 aches, stings, hurtings
10 ",,,they saw that I had been entrusted with ___ task of preaching the gospel to the Gentiles..." (2:7)
11 "...do not grieve the Holy Spirit of God, with ____ you were sealed..." (Eph. 4:30)
12 at once, immediately
14 **Anointed One, Messiah, Son of David, Jesus who came to bring liberty from sin and peace with God and who will come again to bring all things under his control (p. 439)**
16 **hesitating, doubting, uncertain (p. 46)**, puzzled
18 to the point of
20 the thing
22 "I __ not writing this to shame you, but to warn you..." (1 Cor. 4:14)
23 "...attaining to the whole measure __ the fullness of Christ." (Eph. 4:13)
24 given, granted
26 however, on the contrary
27 **boiling, glowing with zeal, a show of affection and devotion (p. 181)**
28 "...we ourselves ___ sinners..." (2:17)
29 "...who makes you different ____ anyone else..." (1 Cor. 4:7)
32 alter, modify, swap, trade, replace
33 near
34 "...so that the truth of the gospel might remain with ___." (2:5)
35 "...we seek to __ justified in Christ..." (2:17)
36 once more
38 a marker that shows purpose or result (2 words)
40 **sons and daughters, offspring, descendants (p. 404)**
41 not any
42 you and me
43 beloved, cherished, treasured, precious

DOWN

2 want, desire
3 shaped, created, produced
4 in no way
5 "until we all reach unity __ the faith..." (Eph. 4:13)
6 persons
7 "...a man __ not justified by observing the law, but by faith in Jesus..." (2:16)
8 "For through the law I died to the law so that I might live ___ God." (2:19)
9 "...false brothers had infiltrated our ranks __ spy on the freedom we have in Christ..." (2:4)
11 at the time
13 gain, secure, attain, accomplish
14 having children
15 those people
17 reason, intention, drive
19 certain ones
21 in excess of, above
25 **shut out, exclude (p. 124)**
30 might, possibly will
31 only; simply
32 might
33 will, decide; wish, desire
35 since
37 **rightness, wellness, correctness (p. 211)**
38 "...you had become __ dear to us." (1 Thes. 2:8)
39 **voice, sound; speaking, language (p. 432)**
44 also, likewise

Galatians 4:17-20

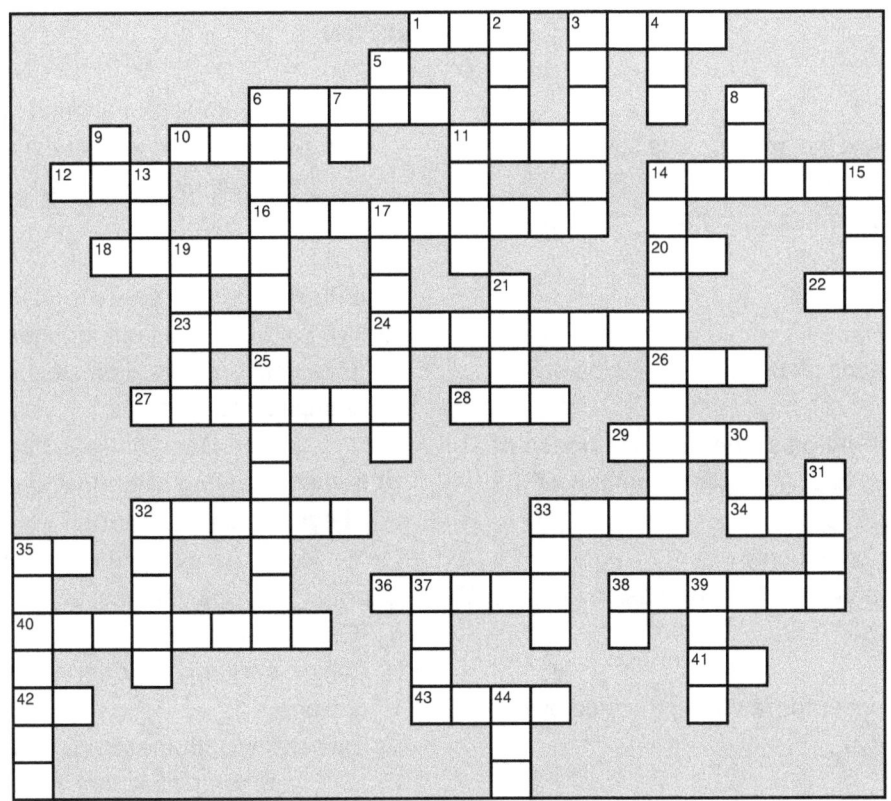

___ ___ ___ ___ ___ ___ ___ ___ ' ___ ___
 5   6   3   7   2   3   3   4   3   3

___ ___ . What they ___ ___ to ___ you ___ , ___ you ___
 2   4   4   2   8   4   2   6 (2 words)   3

___ zealous for ___ . ___ is ___ to be zealous, ___ ___ ___ is good,
 2   4   2   4   8   3   7

___ to be ___ always and ___ ___ ___ I ___ you. My ___
 3   2   3   4   4   2   4

___ , for ___ I am ___ ___ the ___ ___ ___
 8   4   5   2   5   2   10   5

___ is ___ in you, ___ I ___ I ___ be with you ___ and ___ my
 6   6   3   4   5   3   6

___ , ___ I am ___ about you!
 4   7   9

63

Galatians 4:21-23

ACROSS

1. belonging to him
3. "For this ___ how the promise was stated..." (Rom. 9:9)
5. "...Abram gave the name Ishmael __ the son..." (Gen. 16:15)
6. normal, usual, regular
9. the thing
10. through, by means of; because of, for the sake of (4 words)
14. **regulations, principles; the first five books of the Scriptures, or any single command of the Scriptures (p. 279)**
16. below a status or authority
17. servant; person owned as a possession for various lengths of times
20. one plus one
21. "...all who sin under the law will __ judged by the law." (Rom. 2:12)
22. female adult
24. "the LORD did ___ Sarah what he had promised. (Gen. 21:1)
25. assurance, guarantee, pledge
26. "All ___ sin apart from the law will also perish apart from the law..." (Rom. 2:12)
27. brought into the world

DOWN

1. "Sarah became pregnant and bore a son to Abraham in his old age, at the very time God ___ promised him." (Gen. 21:2)
2. child, descendant
3. in a form to be read
4. **children, descendants (p. 413)**
5. say, said, general term for speaking
7. "Now you, brothers, like Isaac, ___ children of promise." (4:28)
8. "___ are the God who sees me..." (Gen. 16:13)
10. **hearing, paying attention, understanding, obeying (p. 13)** (2 words)
11. "So Hagar bore Abram a son, and Abram gave ___ name Ishmael ot the son..." (Gen. 16:15)
12. **female servant, maidservant (p. 299)** (2 words)
13. **unrestricted, liberated (p. 131)**
15. "...it __ through Isaac that your offspring will be reckoned." (Gen. 21:12)
18. *"father of many"* **(p. 1),** father of Isaac
19. "__ other words, it is not the natural children who are God's children..." (Rom. 9:8)
20. "At ____ time the son born in the ordinary way persecuted the son born by the power of the Spirit..." (Gal. 4:29)
23. "Nor because they ___ his descendants are they all Abraham's children." (Rom. 9:7)
27. through

Sadly, there are those who try to turn us in the wrong direction. They want to alienate us from God and His children. Be aware and cautious! What is God saying to you from Galatians? --Jan

Galatians 4:21-23

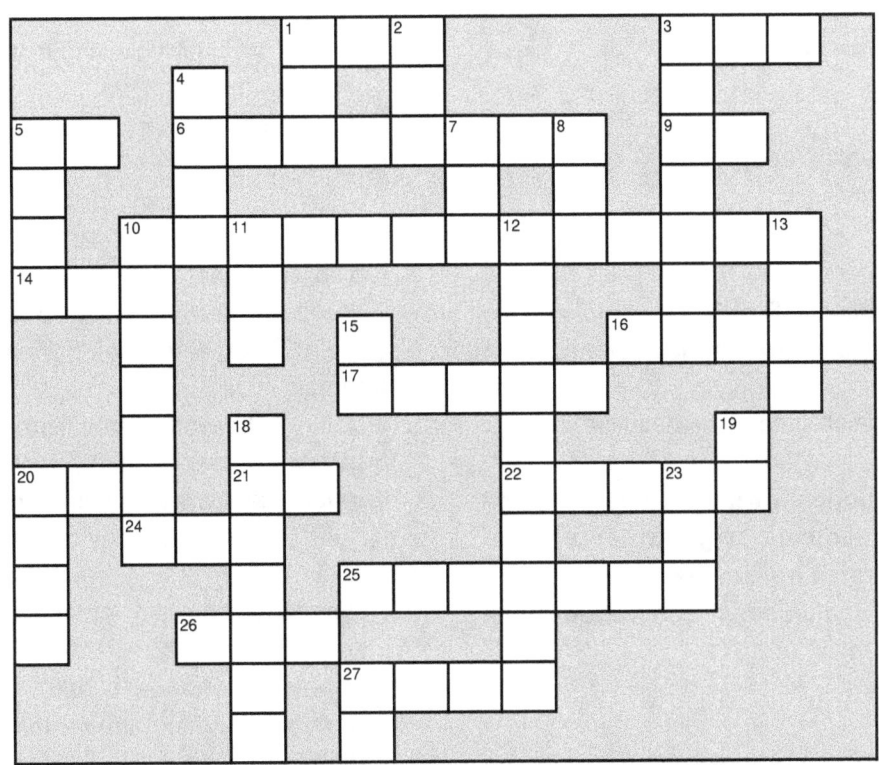

___ me, ___ ___ want ___ ___ ___ ___ ___,
 4   3   3   2   2   5   3   3

___ you not ___ what the law says? ___ ___ ___ ___
 3   7 (2 words)   3   2   2   7

___ ___ ___ ___ ___ , one ___ the
 4   7   3   3   4   2

_____ and the other by the ___ ___ . ___ ___
10 (2 words)   4   5   3   3

by the ___ woman ___ ___ the ___ way; but his son
       5   3   4   8

by the free woman was born _____ a ___ .
                            13 (4 words)   7

65

Galatians 4:24-27

ACROSS

2 **sterile, not bearing children (p. 375)**
4 among
9 one plus one
11 **deserted, lonely (p. 166)**
13 for the reason that
15 female parent
19 "Him ___ overcomes I will make a pillar in the temple of my God..." (Rev. 3:12)
21 **sons, daughters, offspring, descendants (p. 104)**
23 single
26 "...more ___ the children of the desolate woman..." (Isa. 54:1)
27 **speaking allegorically with another meaning, significant in another way (p. 16) (2 words)**
29 **released, liberated from ownership, confinement, and distress; God's release of the sinner from sin (p. 131)**
31 **hill (p. 293)**
32 also, likewise
33 *"Sin [pagan moon god]; glare [from white chalk]"* **(p. 367)**
35 "...he carried me away in the Spirit ___ a mountain..." (Rev. 21:10)
37 current
39 "...all of ___ who were baptized into Christ..." (3:27)
40 female adults
42 belongs to that woman
47 represents (2 words)
48 by means of; out of
50 **gives birth, has sons and/or daughters (p. 79)** (2 words)
53 married man
54 that woman
56 "...what cannot ___ shaken may remain." (Heb. 12:27)
57 might, can
58 **upward, from a higher place, on top (p. 34)**
60 yours and mine

DOWN

1 "...we ___ receiving a kingdom that cannot be shaken..." (Heb. 12:28)
2 on the contrary, however
3 not any
5 "...'Write ___ down, for these words are trustworthy and true.'" (Rev. 21:5)
6 also, likewise
7 "...God __ treating you as sons..." (Heb. 12:7)
8 **life of being a servant, bondage (p. 106)**
10 female adult
12 "...to ___ heavenly Jerusalem..." (Heb. 12:22)
13 **burst; exclaim (p. 359) (2 words)**
14 **solemn agreement; will, testament (p. 96)**
16 "...hold __ the testimony of Jesus." (Rev. 12:17)
17 "For it is written ___ Abraham had two sons..." (Gal. 4:22)
18 **people in bondage (p. 106)**
20 **Sarai's handmaid, the mother of Ishmael (p. 3)**
22 in a form to be read
24 the thing
25 **cry out, exclaim (p. 71) (2 words)**
28 "...They will __ his people..." (Rev. 21:3)
30 stand for, symbolize, characterize
34 at the present time
36 "...the new Jerusalem, which __ coming down out of heaven..." (Rev. 3:12)
38 possesses, holds
41 greater than
43 aches, hurts; sorrow
44 "...I will write on him the name __ my God..." (Rev. 3:12)
45 *"desert"* **(p. 50),** large peninsula that borders the Red Sea, Indian Ocean, Persian Gulf, and Syrian Desert
46 because
49 within
51 town, metropolis
52 **childbirth (p. 282)**
55 contain, possess, experience
59 "...God himself will __ with them and be their God." (Rev. 21:3)

Galatians 4:24-27

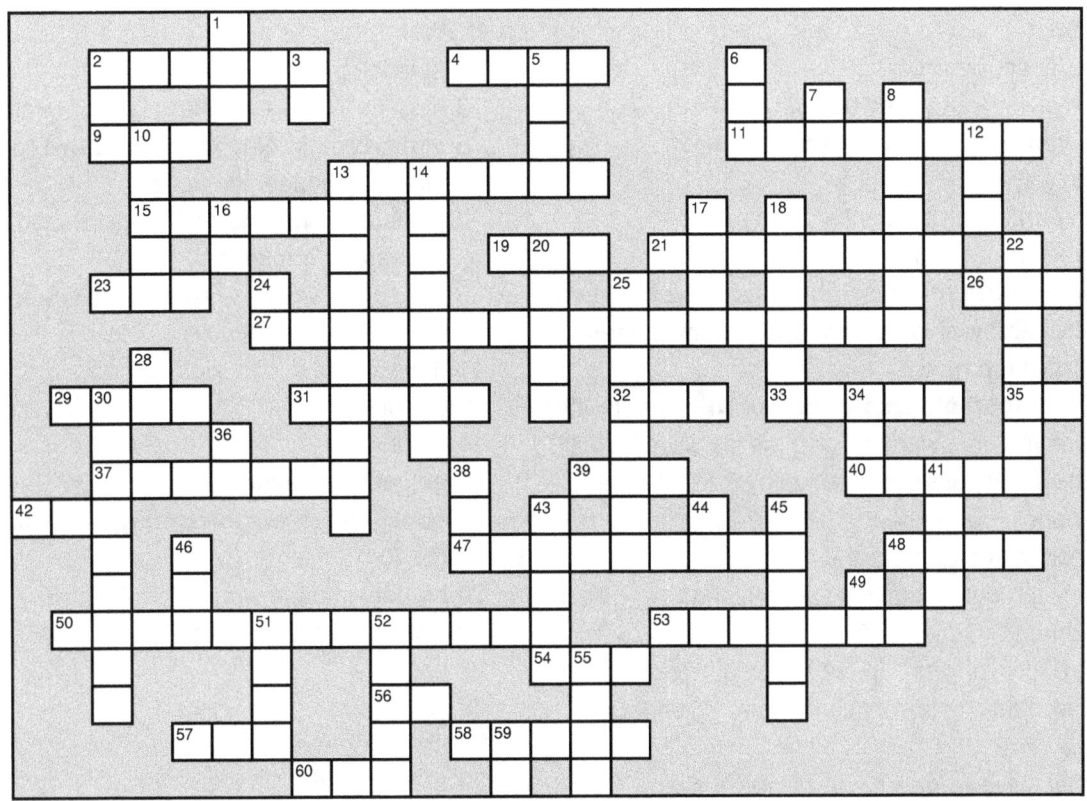

These things ___ ___ _____, ___ ___ ___
            3   2   17 (2 words)   3   3   5

_____ ___ covenants. ___ ___ ___ ___ ___ ___
   9   3   3   8   2   4   5   5

___ _____ ___ ___ ___ ___ ___ : ___ ___
 3 13 (2 words) 3   3   2   2   6   4   2

___ . ___ Hagar _____ Mount Sinai ___ ___ ___ corresponds ___ the
 5   3   9 (2 words)   2   6   3   2

___ ___ ___ Jerusalem, ___ ___ is in ___ ___ ___
 7   4   2   7   3   7   4   3

___ . ___ the Jerusalem ___ is ___ is ___, and she is ___ ___ .
 8   3   4   5   4   3   6

For ___ is ___ : " ___ glad, O ___ ___ who bears ___ children;
     2   7   2   6   5   2

_____ and _____ , ___ who ___ no ___ ___ ; because
10 (2 words)   8 (2 words)   3   4   5   5

___ ___ the children of the ___ woman than of her who ___ no ___ . "
 4   3   8   3   7

67

Galatians 4:28-31

ACROSS

2 also, even, likewise
4 "The law __ not based on faith…" (3:12)
7 assurance, guarantee, agreement, oath
8 in no way
10 take part, receive a portion
12 normal, usual, regular
13 **fellow countrymen, neighbors; fellow believers in the family of faith; regularly refers to men and women (p. 6)**
15 **holy, authoritative collection of writings (p. 82)**
17 "…are you not aware of ____ the law says?" (4:21)
19 "…the sinful passions aroused by the law were __ work in our bodies…" (Rom. 7:5)
20 yet, on the other hand
21 "…it is through Isaac that your offspring ____ be reckoned." (Gen. 21:12)
23 *"he [God] laughs"* **(p. 203),** son of Abraham
24 "All who rely on observing the law ___ under a curse…" (3:10)
25 "…that slave woman's son will never share __ the inheritance…" (Gen. 21:10)
26 **take out, remove; drive out, expel (p. 122)** (3 words)
28 female adult
30 "…are you not aware __ what the law says?" (4:21)
31 child, offspring, descendant
33 **female servant, maidservant (p. 299)** (2 words)
35 method, means, manner
36 "For it is written ____ Abraham had two sons…" (4:22)

DOWN

1 belonging to the adult female
3 "it is sin living in me that ____ it." (Rom. 7:20)
5 **wind, breath, God the Holy Spirit (p. 331)**
6 legacy, birthright, heritage
7 **pursued, systematically oppressed and harassed; chased (p. 104)**
9 "___ promises were spoken to Abraham and to his seed…" (3:16)
11 that woman's
13 through
14 the thing
16 authority, strength, ability
18 **sons, daughters, offspring, descendants (p. 404)**
20 brought into the world
22 in accordance with, as
27 because
28 you and I
29 not at all, in no way
32 at the present time
33 general term for speaking, tell
34 among, in addition to

Again, be aware of those who try to turn us against God and God's children. Trust God's guidance through His Word. A person can't be both for God and against God. Let's be strong and pray for God's wisdom. What is God saying to you from Galatians? --Jan

Galatians 4:28-31

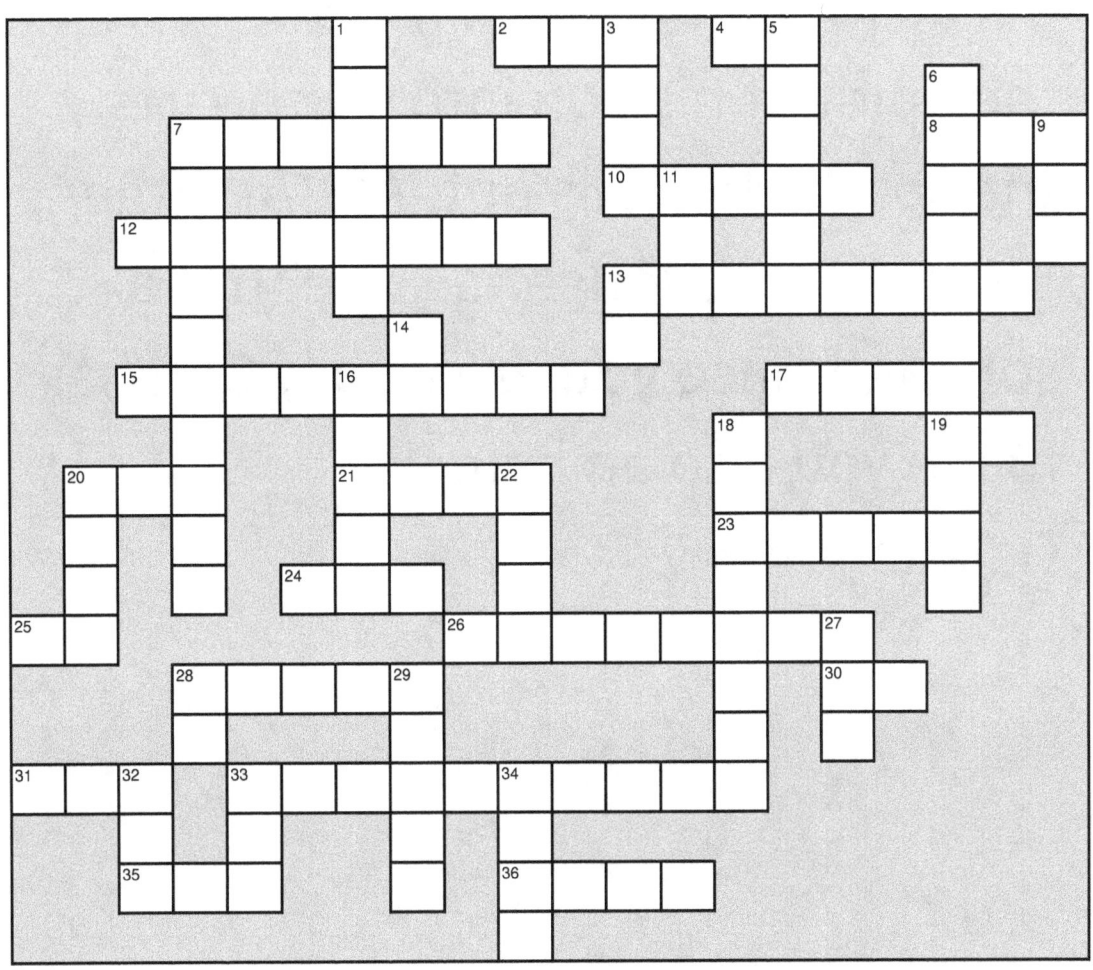

___ you, ___, ___, ___, ___
 3   8   4   5   3   8

___ ___. time ___ ___ ___ ___ the
2   7   2   4   3   3   4   2

___ ___ ___ the son born ___ the ___ of the
 8   3   10   2   5

___. the same now. ___ ___ the ___ the ___
6 2 2   3   4   4   9

___ ? " ___ the ___ ___ son, ___ the
 3   8 (3 words) 10 (2 words) 3   3   3

slave woman's son ___ ___ ___ in the ___
                   4   5   5   11

___ the free ___ son." Therefore, brothers, ___ are ___ children of the slave
 4   6   2   3

___, but of the free woman.
 5

69

Because you are his sons, God sent the Spirit of his Son into our hearts, the spirit who calls out, ABBA, father. So you are no longer a slave, but a son; and since you are a son, God has made you also an heir.
Galatians 4:6-7

Galatians 5:1

ACROSS

2 "...you also died to the law through the body __ Christ..." (Rom. 7:4)
4 **frame and cross bar placed on draft animals ensuring service (p. 183)**
5 you and me
8 "__ on your guard; stand firm in the faith..." (1 Cor. 16:13)
9 "They tie up heavy loads and put them on men's shoulders, but they themselves ___ not willing to lift a finger to move them." (Matt. 23:4)
10 **be constant, persevere (p. 204) (2 words)**
13 **life of being a servant, bondage (p. 106)**
15 in no way
16 the thing
17 **liberty, being unrestricted or not enslaved (p. 131)**

DOWN

1 "...But __ not use your freedom to indulge the sinful nature..." (5:13)
3 **liberated, unbound, released, (p. 132)**
4 you personally
6 place, establish
7 also, even, likewise
8 loaded, weighed down, troubled
11 "The one who sent me is with me; he ___ not left me alone..." (John 8:29)
12 through
14 allow
16 "...We believe it __ through the grace of our Lord Jesus that we are saved..." (Acts 15:11)
17 "He made no distinction between us and them, __ he purified their hearts by faith." (Acts 15:9)

___ ___ ___
2   2   3

_____ that Christ ___
     7   3

___ ___ ___.
 3   2   4

_____ , then, ___
   9 (2 words)   3

___ _____ again ___ a
 2   8   2

___ ___ _____.
 4   2   7

Galatians 5:2-6

ACROSS

3 entire
5 **testify; affirm (p. 259)**
8 expect, look forward to, anticipate
10 you and I
11 **kindness and favor toward someone (p. 433)**
12 "...for __ the proper time we will reap a harvest if we do not give up." (6:9)
14 human being, person
15 all, each
17 **practice (p. 333);** mind, comply with
19 "For everything ____ was written in the past was written to teach us..." (Rom. 15:4)
21 general term for speaking
23 "...God has shown me that I should not call ___ man impure or unclean." (Acts 10:28)
24 allows, permits, agrees to
26 you personally
28 "All ___ rely on observing the law are under a curse..." (3:10)
31 "___ in this hope we were saved..." (Rom. 8:24)
32 "...judgment without mercy will be shown to anyone who has not ____ merciful..." (James 2:13)
33 indicate
35 *"little;"* **apostle to the Gentiles (p. 313),** author of Galatians
37 not
39 the thing personally
40 "...His letters contain some things that ___ hard to understand..." (2 Pet. 3:16)
41 **vindicated, declared righteous, in a proper relationship with God (p. 102)**
44 "...do not let yourselves be burdened again by a yoke __ slavery." (5:1)
46 once more
47 the surgical process which was originally the sign of the covenant between Abraham and God
49 dropped, tumbled, gone down
50 "...The one who __ throwing you into confusion will pay the penalty..."(5:10)
51 and not
52 "...live by the Spirit, and you ____ not gratify the desires of the sinful nature." (5:16)
54 "For whoever keeps ___ whole law and yet stumbles at just one point is guilty of breaking all of it." (James 2:10)

ACROSS (continued)

56 not any
57 "This righteousness from God comes _____ faith..." (Rom. 3:22)
58 statement, declaration

DOWN

1 "___ if you are led by the Spirit, you are not under law." (5:18)
2 "You, my brothers, were called to __ free..." (5:13)
3 "...there is no other name under heaven given to men by _____ we must be saved." (Acts 4:12)
4 allow, permit, agree to
6 matters, is important
7 **what is right, justice, doing what is in agreement with God's standards, being in proper relationship with God (p. 102)**
8 absent, gone missing
9 you and I
12 "What has happened to ___ your joy..." (4:15)
13 that man, that person
14 belonging to me
16 **profit, usefulness, benefit (p. 296)**
17 one
18 "...so that you may not be carried away __ the error of lawless men..." (2 Pet. 3:17)
20 had the surgical process done which was originally the sign of the covenant between Abraham and God
22 **generosity, kindness, being devloted (p. 2)**
25 **wind, breath, God the Holy Spirit (p. 331)**
27 **acting out (p. 139)**
29 **expect with confidence (p. 133)**
30 compelled, required
34 no surgical process which was originally the sign of the covenant between Abraham and God
36 on condition that
38 "Circumcision ___ value if you observe the law..." (Rom. 2:25)

Galatians 5:2-6

DOWN (Continued)

41 **Joshua, "*Yahweh saves*" (p. 200)**
42 enthusiastically, impatiently
43 "Make every effort to live __ peace with all men..." (Heb. 12:14)
45 "Christ redeemed us ____ the curse of the law..." (3:13)
46 separated, divided
48 **Anointed One, Messiah, Son of David, Jesus who came to bring liberty from sin and peace with God and who will come again to bring all things under his control (p. 439)**
49 **trust, the Christian system of belief and lifestyle (p. 314)**
53 **regulations, principles; the first five books of the Scriptures, or any single command of the Scriptures (p. 279)**
55 "...do not use your freedom __ indulge the sinful nature..." (5:13)

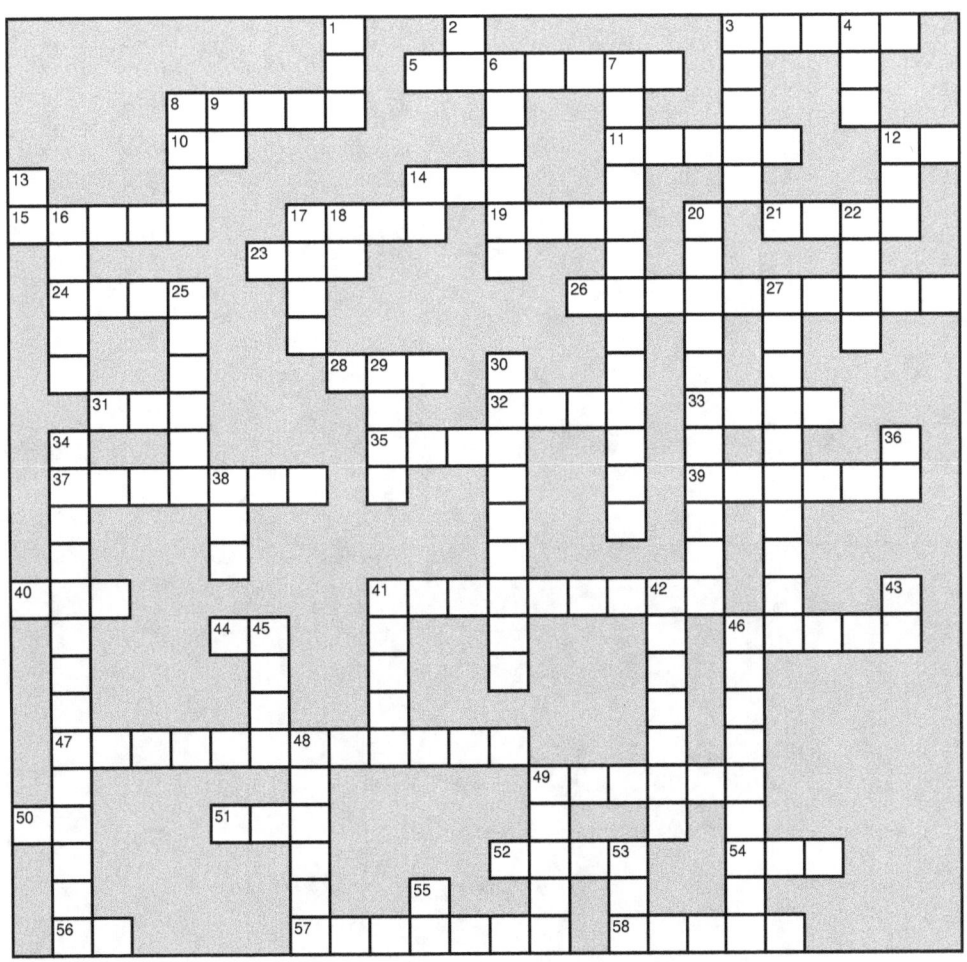

Those people are zealous to win you over, but for no good. What they want is to alienate you from us, so that you may be zealous for them. It is fine to be zealous, provided the purpose is good. Galatians 4:17-18

Galatians 5:2-6

___ ___ ___ ! I, ___, ___ you ___ ___ you ___ ___ ___
 4   2   5   4   4   4   2   3   10   2

___ ___ ___ be ___ ___ ___ ___ you ___ ___.
 11   6   4   2   2   5   2   2   3

___ I ___ to ___ ___ ___ himself be circumcised that ___
 5   7   5   3   3   4   2

___ ___ to ___ ___ ___ ___. You who ___ trying to be
 2   9   4   3   5   3   3

___ ___ law have ___ ___ Christ; you have ___ ___
 9   2   4   9   6   4

from ___. ___ ___ ___ ___ ___ ___ ___ the
      5   3   2   5   2   7   5   7

___ the ___ ___ ___ ___. For ___ Christ ___
 6   13   3   5   2   2   5

___ ___ ___ ___ ___ ___ value. The
 7   12   3   14   3   3

___ thing that ___ is faith ___ ___ through ___.
 4   6   10   6   4

Remember, circumcision represents being saved by the law/works from the first covenant versus being saved by faith in the new covenant from Jesus Christ. And, faith and love go hand in hand. What is God saying to you from Galatians? --Jan

Galatians 5:7-12

ACROSS

7 influence, advice
8 "..._____ sows sparingly will also reap sparingly..." (2 Cor. 9:6)
10 those people
11 that person; him
13 reserved, set aside
15 contest, competition, battle, pursuit
17 operates
19 **hindered, stopped, impeded progress** (3 words)
20 might
21 "...the son born __ the ordinary way persecuted the son born by the power of the Spirit..." (4:29)
22 "I do all this for the sake __ the gospel..." (1 Cor. 9:23)
25 "...Evidently some people are throwing you ____ confusion..." (1:7)
26 "I have ____ crucified with Christ and I no longer live, but Christ lives in me..." (Gal. 2:20)
28 minding, following, observing
30 "I am astonished ____ you are so quickly deserting the one who called you by the grace of Christ..." (Gal. 1:6)
32 "...the Spirit intercedes for the saints in accordance with God's _____." (Rom. 8:27)
36 "Who shall separate us ____ the love of Christ..." (Rom. 8:35)
37 again, even now
39 "You foolish Galatians! ___ has bewitched you..." (Gal. 3:1)
40 want, desire
41 "...I __ perplexed about you!" (Gal. 4:20)
42 "___ the foolishness of God is wiser than man's wisdom..." (1 Cor. 1:25)
43 **pursued, systematically oppressed and harassed, chased**
44 mixture that's ready to bake
45 might
46 entire
49 **situation, set of circumstances**
51 you and I
52 "...what was promised, _____ given through faith in Jesus Christ, might be given to those who believe." (3:22)
53 "I __ astonished that you are so quickly deserting the one who called you..." (Gal. 1:6)
54 additional, extra, further
55 **leaven**
56 small amount of
57 also
58 "Now that faith ___ come, we are no longer under the supervision of the law." (3:25)
60 convinced, persuaded; trusting in
59 "You who are trying __ be justified by law have been alienated from Christ..." (5:4)
65 "The promises ____ spoken to Abraham and to his seed..." (Gal. 3:16)
66 **reality**

DOWN

1 "Therefore, __ we have opportunity, let us do good to all people..." (6:10)
2 "...Forgetting what __ behind and straining toward what is ahead," (Phil. 3:13)
3 "...I had confidence __ all of you..." (2 Cor. 2:3)
4 "Do ___ not know that in a race all the runners run, but only one gets the prize..." (1 Cor. 9:24)
5 "I wrote as I did so that when I came I should not __ distressed by those who ought to make me rejoice..." (2 Cor. 2:3)
6 "...He will remind you of my ___ of life in Christ Jesus..." (1 Cor. 4:17)
7 **proclaiming, lecturing, speaking**
9 **opinion, attitude**
10 assume, hold
12 in no way
13 type, sort, form
14 **judgment, condemnation; sentence, punishment**
15 **striving, giving effort;** going fast on your two legs and feet
16 originate, arrive, happen
18 **stumbling block, obstacle; something that causes sin**
23 not any
24 **nullified, made ineffective**
27 "...God works for ___ good of those who love him..." (Rom. 8:28)
29 lump, lot, bunch
31 "...Don't you know that a little yeast works _____ the whole batch of dough?" (I Cor. 5:6)
32 "You ___ are trying to be justified by law have been alienated from Christ..." (5:4)
33 **wooden instrument of torture; symbolic representation of redemption**
34 **cut off,** weaken, render impotent and powerless
35 surgical process which was originally the sign of the covenant between Abraham and God
38 **master**
43 **carry, bear, tolerate, help, support**
46 "...God _____ justify the Gentiles by faith..." (3:8)
47 "...that too God will make clear to you." (Phil. 3:15)
48 **people who cause trouble or start revolts**
49 **invites, summons**
50 "...I am not free from God's law but am under Christ's law..." (1 Cor. 9:21)
51 for what reason
52 **fellow countrymen, neighbors; fellow believers in the family of faith; regularly refers to men and women**
61 single person, less than two
62 on condition that
63 "...Run in such a way as to get ___ prize." (1 Cor. 9:24)
64 "...know ___ depth of my love for you." (2 Cor. 2:4)

Galatians 5:7-12

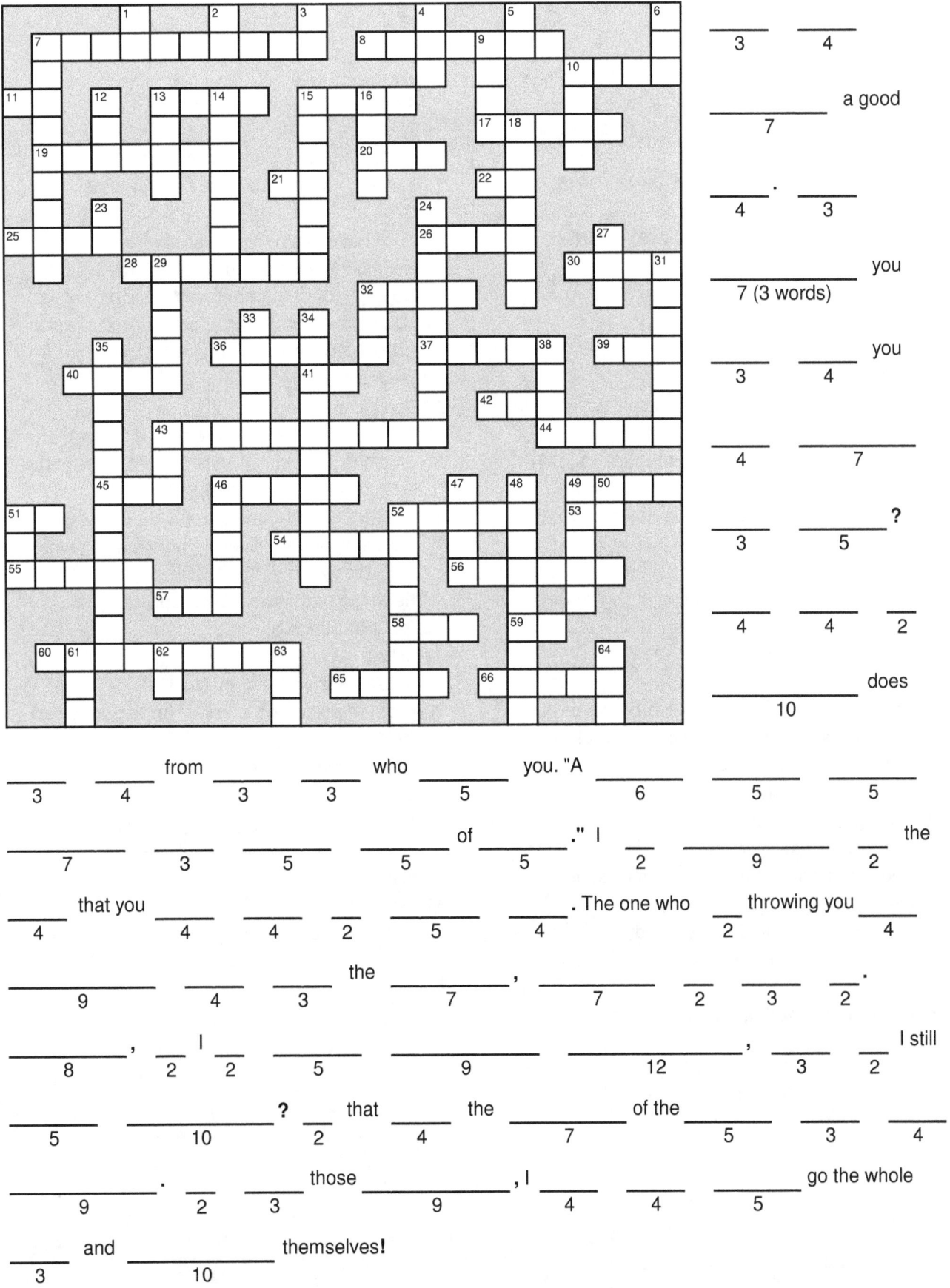

Galatians 5:13-15

ACROSS

1. "...by doing good ___ should silence the ignorant talk of foolish men." (1 Pet. 2:15)
2. "Before this faith came, we ____ held prisoners by the law..." (3:23)
3. "...we were held prisoners __ the law..." (3:23)
5. you personally
8. **word spoken or written (p. 249)**, directive, order, instruction
10. but, instead, yet, except
12. you and I
13. also
14. whole
16. "...but __ not use your freedom as a cover-up for evil..." (1 Pet. 2:16)
18. **fulfilled, made full; made complete (p. 329)** (2 words)
20. **generosity, kindness, being devloted (p. 2)**
21. in no way
22. on condition that
23. "Carry each other's burdens, and __ this way you will fulfill the law of Christ." (6:2)
24. **liberated, not enslaved (p. 131)**
26. one
27. **regulation, principle; first five books of the Scriptures, or any single command of the Scriptures (p. 279)**
28. each other (2 words)
29. sinking your teeth into
32. "Be careful, however, that the exercise of your freedom does not become a stumbling block __ the weak." (1 Cor. 8:9)
33. "...no one ever hated his own body, but he feeds and cares for it, just as Christ does ___ church" (Eph. 5:29)
35. **consumed, used up (p. 23)**

DOWN

1. belonging to you
2. **beware, pay attention (p. 71)** (2 words)
3. however
4. "...some false brothers had infiltrated our ranks to spy __ the freedom we have in Christ Jesus..." (2:4)
5. "___ have heard that it was said, 'Love your neighbor and hate your enemy.'" (Mat. 5:43)
6. **liberty, not being enslaved (p. 131)**
7. "Do not seek revenge __ bear a grudge against one of your people..." (Lev. 19:18)
9. belonging to me
11. continue
12. "...The righteous ____ live by faith." (3:11)
15. "And the second __ like it: 'Love your neighbor as yourself.'" (Mat. 22:39)
16. **eating up, consuming, injuring (p. 223)**
17. "...do not let yourselves __ burdened again by a yoke of slavery." (5:1)
18. **flesh, passion and frailty, spritually low (p. 363)** (2 words)
19. utilize, apply
21. **those near or close by (p. 330)**
22. **provide a starting point or opportunity for (p. 63)**
25. one another (2 words)
26. **act as a slave for (p. 107)**
30. "Those who belong __ Christ Jesus have crucified the sinful nature..." (5:24)
31. also
34. like

Galatians 5:13-15

___ , ___ brothers, ___ called ___ . ___ ___ ___ ___ ___ ___
 3   2   4   2   2   4   3   2   3   3   4

___ ___ ___ ___ ___ , ___
 7   2   7   3 12(2 words) 6 5

___ ___ ___ . The ___ ___ ___ ___ in a ___
10 (2 words) 2 4   6   3   2 8 (2 words)   6

___ : "Love your ___ ___ ___ ." ___ ___ ___ ___
 7   8   2   8   2   3   4   2

___ ___ ___ ___ , ___ you ___ be
 6   3   9 9 (2 words) 8 (2 words) 2   4

___ ___ each other.
 9   2

Galatians 5:16-18

ACROSS

1 "...When I want to do good, evil __ right there with me." (Rom. 7:21)
3 "Those who belong to Christ Jesus have crucified the sinful nature ____ its passions and desires." (5:24)
4 "...those who live in accordance with the Spirit have their minds set on ____ the Spirit desires." (Rom. 8:5)
5 **walk, conduct your life (p. 320)**
7 **to be an opponent (p. 32)** (2 words)
11 "...those who ___ led by the Spirit of God are sons of God." (Rom. 8:14)
13 will, decide; wish, desire
15 **wind, breath, God the Holy Spirit (p. 331)**
16 below the authority of
20 **flesh, passion and frailty, spritually low (p. 363)** (2 words)
22 "The acts of the sinful nature ___ obvious..." (5:19)
23 "I __ not understand what I do..." (Rom. 7:15)
24 "...through Christ Jesus ___ law of the Spirit of life set me free..." (Rom. 8:2)
25 rather
27 general term for speaking, tell
28 "The mind __ sinful man is death..." (Rom. 8:6)
29 "For sin shall not be your master, because ___ are not under law, but under grace." (Rom. 6:14)

DOWN

2 in order (2 words)
3 "All who sin apart from the law ____ also perish apart from the law..." (Rom. 2:12)
4 "...those who live like this ____ not inherit the kingdom of God." (5:21)
6 one another (2 words)
8 because
9 against, opposed (2 words)
10 **regulations, principles; the first five books of the Scriptures, or any single command of the Scriptures (p. 279)**
12 in no way
14 "___, however, are controlled not by the sinful nature..." (Rom. 8:9)
15 therefore
17 **longings, lustings (p. 156)**
18 on condition that
19 **finish, complete, fulfill (p. 401);** please
21 **brought; paying attention to, listening to (p. 5)**
25 "Since we live __ the Spirit, let us keep in step with the Spirit." (5:25)
26 those things

Let's be careful about getting distracted from faith and love. When we allow other beliefs in, it may only increase and get worse. Let's guard ourselves against temptation and choose to live by the guidance of the Holy Spirit that dwells within us to help us. The Holy Spirit makes us new and full of love, which in turn leads us to good works as an expression of gratitude and love. What is God saying to you from Galatians? --Jan

Galatians 5:16-18

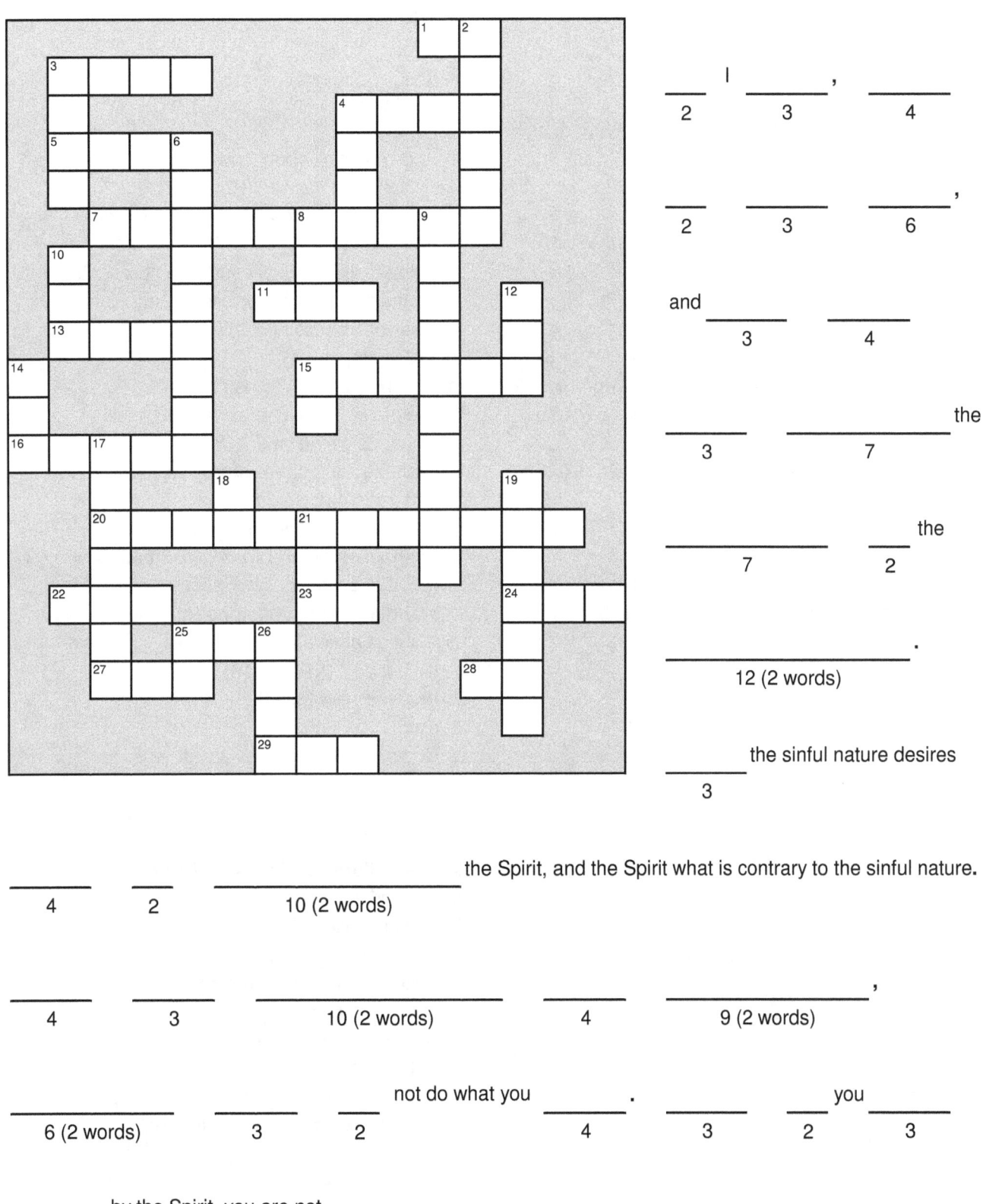

Galatians 5:19-21

ACROSS

1 sects (religious parties), heresies; sacrilege
4 visible, clear, plain, known
8 **magic and enchantment, often involving drugs (p. 423)**
9 what is similar
16 **the one true God (p. 193)**
17 "...rescue us from ___ present evil age..." (1:4)
18 **acquire (p. 233)**
19 **act, practice (p. 339)**
20 **envy (p. 181)**
21 "Formerly, when you ___ not know God..." (4:8)
22 **making enemies and discord, alienation (p. 179)**
24 **fornication, adultery, incest (p. 337)** (2 words)
28 like
30 "...from ___ nature will reap destruction..." (6:8)
31 **outrageous behavior (p. 55)**
34 being intoxicated
36 certain people
37 **revelry (p. 245);** partying, riotous behavior
38 "...the kingdom prepared for ___ since the creation of the world." (Mat. 25:34)
40 tell beforehand
41 also
43 **wrath, fury, anger (p. 197)** (3 words)

DOWN

2 also
3 in no way
5 in the past
6 "...do not think about how to gratify the desires ___ the sinful nature." (Rom. 13:14)
7 "For out of ___ heart come evil thoughts..." (Mat. 15:19)
8 "...the King ___ say to those on his right, 'Come, you who are blessed by my Father; take your inheritance...'" (Mat. 25:34)
10 realm, empire
11 **worship of idols (p. 117)**
12 "Before ___ faith came, we were held prisoners by the law..." (3:23)
13 interested or focused mostly on your own goals and desires (2 words)
14 jealousy, greed, desire, resentment, spite
15 **flesh, passion and frailty, spritually low (p. 363)** (2 words)
23 **standing apart, divisions (p. 103)**
25 "...All other sins a man commits ___ outside his body..." (1 Cor. 6:18)
26 **uncleanness (p. 11)**
27 also
29 works, deeds, activities, tasks, jobs
32 also
33 "...watch out or ___ will be destroyed by each other." (5:15)
34 **altercations, strife, quarreling (p. 166)**
35 you and me
39 "...do not use your freedom to indulge ___ sinful nature..." (5:13)
40 "...he ___ sins sexually sins against his own body..." (1 Cor. 6:18)
42 "...your body is a temple ___ the Holy Spirit..." (1 Cor. 6:19)
44 "...the one who sows to please ___ Spirit, from the Spirit will reap eternal life." (6:8)

Galatians 5:19-21

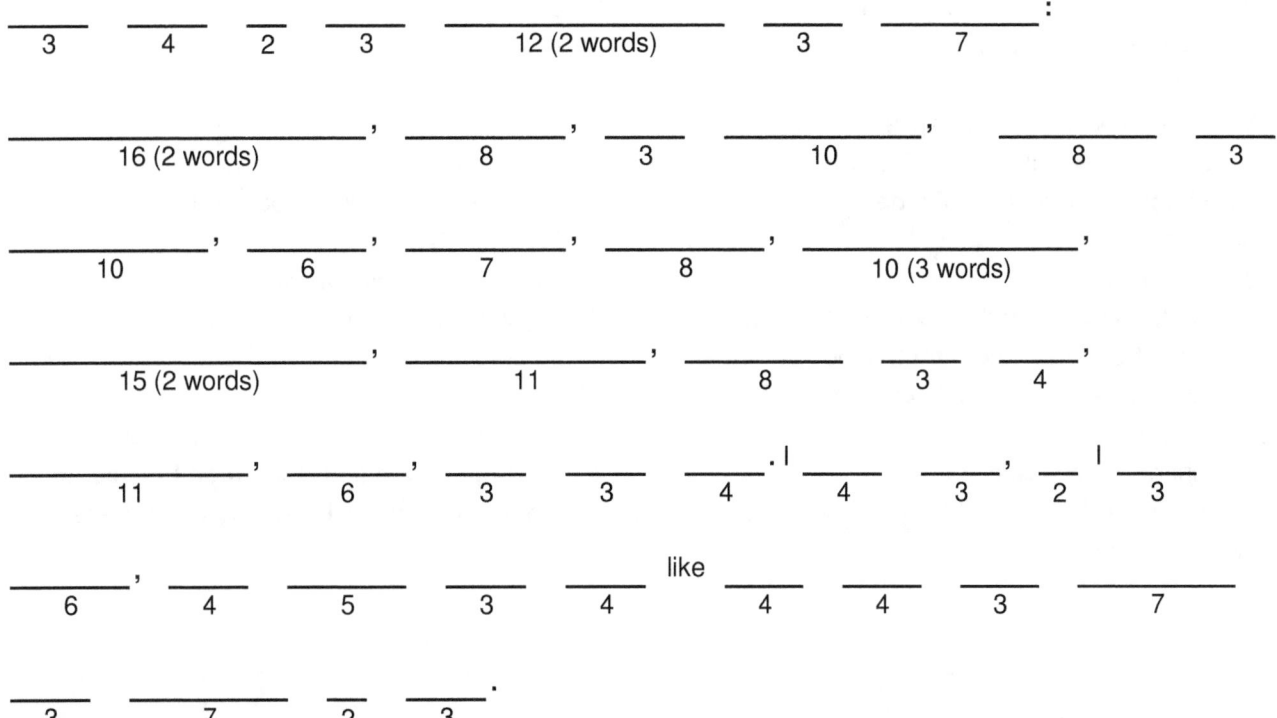

Galatians 5:22-26

ACROSS

1 "...clothe yourselves ____ compassion, kindness, humility, gentleness and patience." (Col. 3:12)
6 similar
8 decency, kindness, honesty, integrity, righteousness
9 **forbearance, internal and external control in a difficult circumstance**
11 "...but __ humility consider others better than yourselves." (Phil. 2:3)
12 characteristics (objects)
13 **harmony, tranquility; safety, welfare, health**
15 "...the sinful nature desires what __ contrary to the Spirit…" (5:17)
16 come into existence as
17 "_____ will be trouble and distress for every human being who does evil…" (Rom. 2:9)
18 **trust, the Christian system of belief and lifestyle**
21 not any
23 "...the Spirit what __ contrary to the sinful nature…" (5:17)
25 pace, stride, movement, action
27 you and me
28 willpower, restraint, strength of mind or will
30 have a relationship; are own by
32 also
35 "...forgive whatever grievances you may ____ against one another…" (Col. 3:13)
36 **rejoicing, happiness, gladness**
37 in no way
38 **goodness**
39 **wind, breath, God the Holy Spirit**
42 **regulation, principle; first five books of the Scriptures, or any single command of the Scriptures**
43 contrary to, opposed
44 you and me
45 being jealous of

DOWN

1 you and I
2 certain people
3 "...I live by faith in the Son of God, ___ loved me and gave himself for me." (Gal. 2:20)
4 allow
5 stay, remain, continue, persist
7 **state of pride**
8 **meekness, humility**
9 obsessions, infatuations, crazes
10 put to death by being nailed to a cross
12 "Every tree that does not bear good fruit is cut down and thrown into ___ fire." (Matt. 7:19)
14 **Anointed One, Messiah, Son of David, Jesus who came to bring liberty from sin and peace with God and who will come again to bring all things under his control**
16 on the other hand
19 **crop, harvest, produce of vegetation**
20 **humankind, with a focus on the fallen human character, which is frail and corrupt in contrast to immaterial (spiritual) things** (2 words)
22 additional
24 because
26 **challenging**
29 exist, reside, dwell, breathe
31 also
33 **longings; cravings, lustings**
34 "__ their fruit you will recognize them…" (Matt. 7:16)
36 **Joshua, "*Yahweh saves*"**
40 "...you have taken off your old self with ___ practices" (Col. 3:9)
41 also
42 **active emotion of God for his Son and his people, and the active emotion his people are to have for God, each other, and even enemies**

Galatians 5:22-26

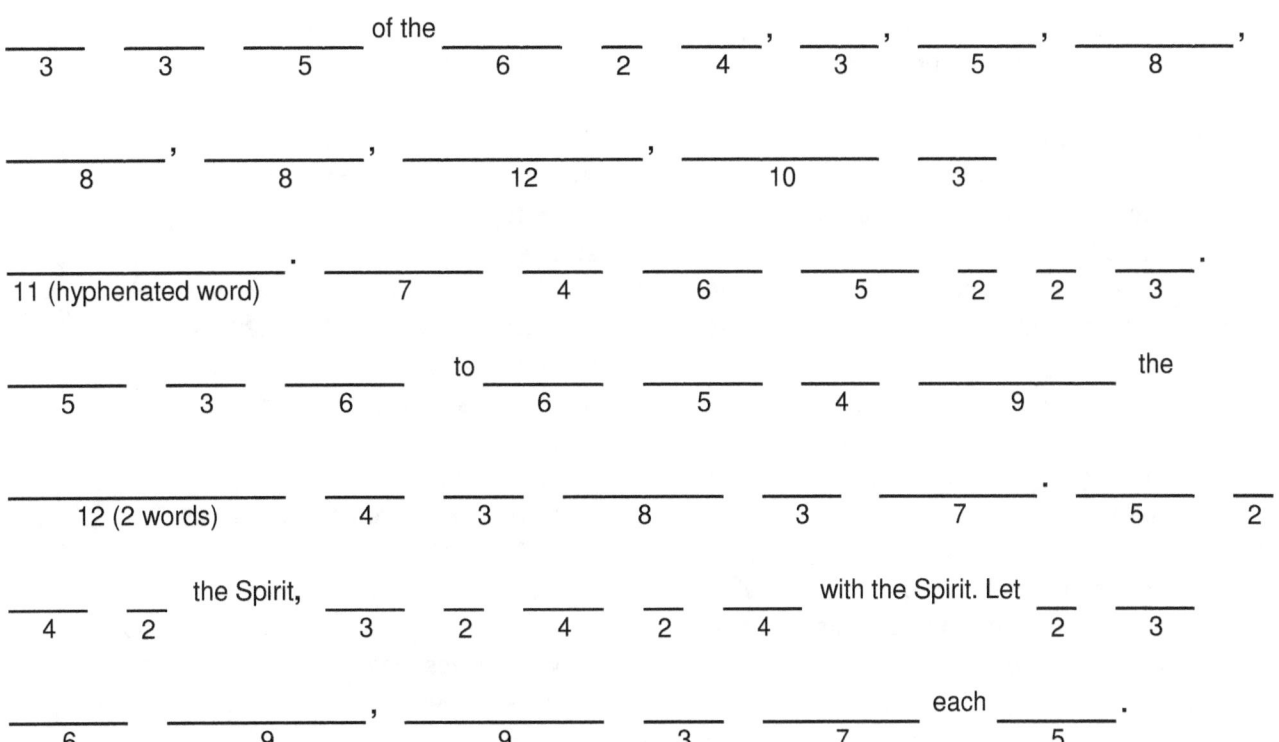

Galatians 6:1-5

ACROSS

1 "...forgive and comfort him, so that he will not __ overwhelmed by excessive sorrow.." (2 Cor. 2:7)
2 devoid of, lacking
6 "___ spiritual man makes judgments about all things…" (1 Cor. 2:15)
7 **Anointed One, Messiah, Son of David, Jesus who came to bring liberty from sin and peace with God and who will come again to bring all things under his control (p. 439)**
9 someone different (2 words)
13 "...he himself __ not subject to any man's judgment." (1 Cor. 2:15)
15 a single person
16 "...show him his fault, just between the two __ you…" (Mat. 18:15)
18 personal
19 contrasting, measuring up, putting side by side
20 **examine (p. 105)**
21 **burden, cargo (p. 424)**
22 **considers, regards, actions of the mind and heart for processing information into understanding and choices (p. 104)**
24 on condition that
25 **be attentive, beware (p. 370)**
26 however
28 **reinstate to a previous condition (p. 220)**
32 **something to boast about; joy (p. 226)**
34 likewise
35 **meekly, kindly (p. 340)**
38 works, deeds, tasks, jobs
40 is able to, knows how to, is capable of
42 at that time
43 "When they measure themselves by themselves and compare themselves with themselves, they ___ not wise." (2 Cor. 10:12)
46 "If you really keep the royal law found __ Scripture, 'Love your neighbor as yourself,' you are doing right." (James 2:8)
47 single person
48 any person
49 **regulations, principles; the first five books of the Scriptures, or any single command of the Scriptures (p. 279)**

DOWN

1 **weight of difficulties (p. 66)**
2 "...live by the Spirit, and you ____ not gratify the desires of the sinful nature." (5:16)
3 that man (person)
4 "...so as __ win those not having the law." (1 Cor. 9:21)
5 "___ by the grace given me I say to every one of you: Do not think of yourself more highly than you ought…" (Rom. 12:3)
6 **tried (p. 314)**
7 overtaken; detected
8 **wrongdoing; any act contrary to the will and law of God (p. 305)**
10 **fellow countrymen, neighbors; fellow believers in the family of faith; regularly refers to men and women (p. 6)**
11 one another's (2 words)
12 one, anyone, anything; some, someone
14 religious and holy or saintly
15 "...watch out __ you will be destroyed by each other." (5:15)
17 **observe fully, keep (p. 25)**
20 have, hold, keep
23 "...If any one of you thinks he __ wise by the standards of this age, he should become a fool so that he may become wise." (1 Cor. 3:18)
25 "Those ___ belong to Christ Jesus have crucified the sinful nature…" (5:24)
27 "The acts of the sinful nature ___ obvious…" (5:19)
29 every
30 "Before ____ faith came, we were held prisoners by the law…" (3:23)
31 some person
33 misleads, tricks, misinforms
34 also, likewise
36 you personally
37 "...worldly—mere infants __ Christ." (1 Cor. 3:1)
39 no one, not anyone, nobody
41 "Formerly, ____ you did not know God, you were slaves to those who by nature are not gods." (4:8)

Galatians 6:1-5

DOWN (continued)
44 belonging to him (a person)
45 that man (person)
47 personal

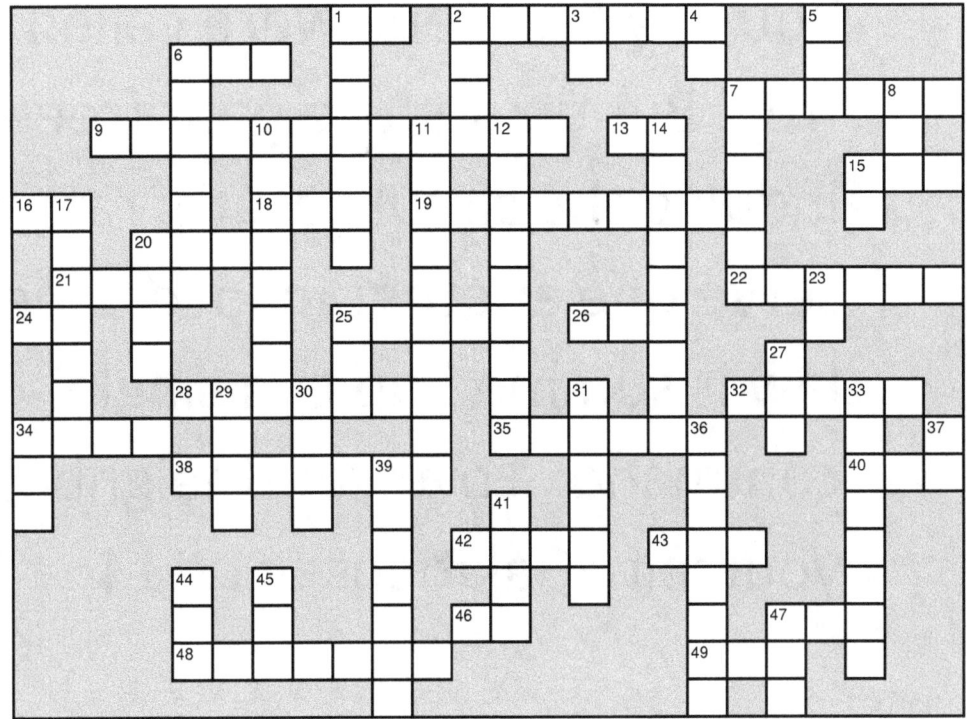

___ , ___ ___ ___ ___ a ___ , you ___ ___
 8   2   7   2   6   2   3   3   3

___ should ___ ___ ___ ___ .
 9   7   3   6   3   5

___ , ___ you ___ may ___ . Carry _____ , ___ ,
 8   2   4   2   7   10 (2 words)   7

___ ___ ___ way you ___ ___ ___ ___ ___ ___ . If
 3   2   4   4   7   3   3   2   6

___ ___ ___ ___ he is ___ , he ___
 6   6   2   2   4   7   8

himself. ___ ___ should ___ ___ ___ ___ . ___ he
          4   3   4   3   3   7   4   3

___ ___ in himself, ___ ___ himself ___ _____
 4   5   7   9   2   12 (2 words)

___ each ___ should carry his ___ ___ .
 3   3   3   4

87

You, my brothers, were called to be free. But do not use your freedom to indulge the sinful nature; rather, serve one another in love. The entire law is summed up in a single command: Love your neighbor as yourself. Galatians 5:13-14

Galatians 6:6

ACROSS

1 **spoken or written communication (p. 249)**
3 every
4 **information (p. 225)**
6 "...let us keep in step ____ the Spirit." (5:25)
7 "...Then he can take pride __ himself, without comparing himself to somebody else," (6:4)
8 **communicate (p. 235)**
9 should
11 generic for points, ideas, features, details
13 "...the Lord has commanded that those ___ preach the gospel should receive their living from the gospel." (1 Cor. 9:14)

DOWN

1 **spoken or written communication (p. 249)**
2 gets
3 some person
4 **one who informs others (p. 225)**
5 belonging to him (a person)
10 "The elders who direct ___ affairs of the church well are worthy of double honor…" (1 Tim. 5:17)
12 **profitable, generous, beneficial, upright, virtuous (p. 2)**

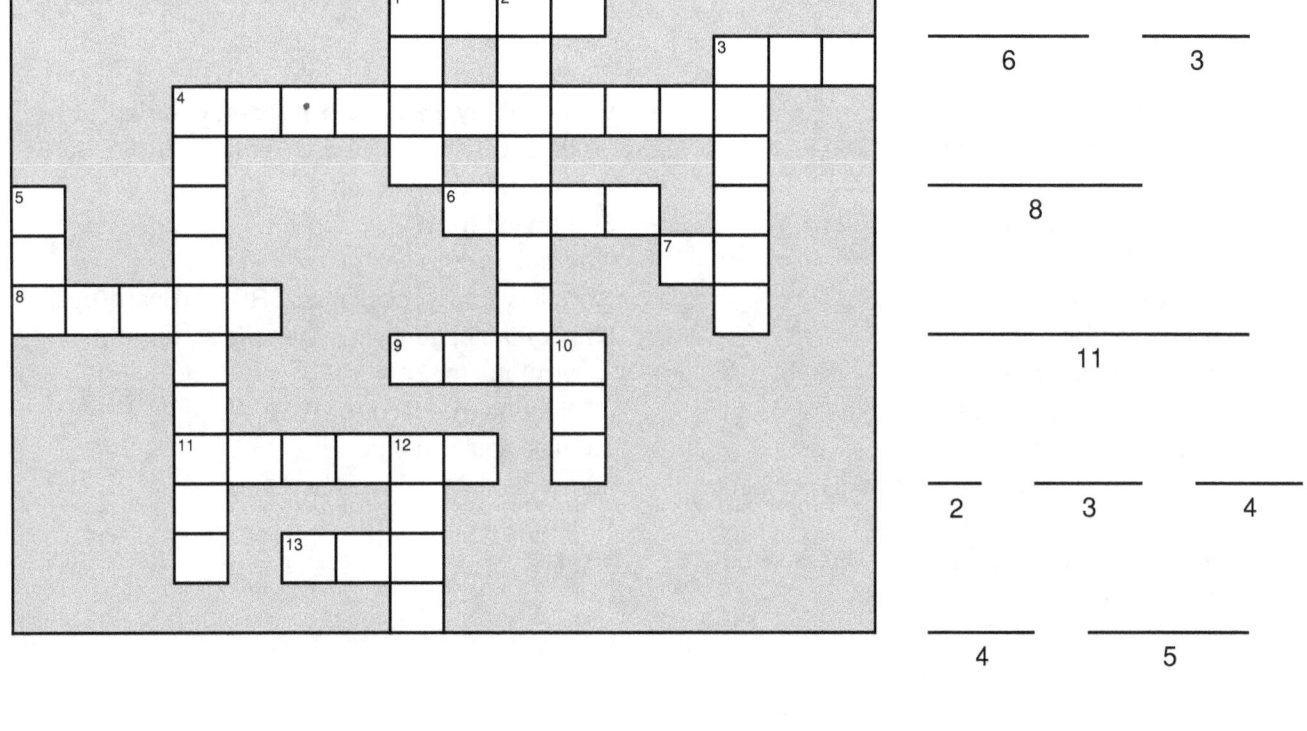

89

Galatians 6:7-10

ACROSS

1 on condition that
3 satisfy, make happy, delight, thrill, entertain
10 consequently
11 "...you know ____ your labor in the Lord is not in vain." (1 Cor. 15:58)
13 right, prime, personal
14 "...The stalk has no head; it ____ produce no flour..." (Hos. 8:7)
15 "...Be faithful, even to the point of death, and I will give you the crown __ life." (Rev. 2:10)
17 **humankind, with a focus on the fallen human character, which is frail and corrupt in contrast to immaterial (spiritual) things (p. 363)** (2 words)
20 "...it is time ___ judgment to begin with the family of God..." (1 Pet. 4:17)
22 **become despondent or faint-hearted (p. 112)** (2 words)
24 "...reap ___ fruit of unfailing love... (Hos. 10:12)
25 you and me
27 **spiritual ruin (p. 425)**
28 particularly
29 "...But watch yourself, __ you also may be tempted." (6:1)
31 you and I
32 hold, keep
33 occasion, instance, moment
34 single person
35 **become weary or exhausted; faint (p. 126)** (2 words)
36 existence, being
37 making, practicing, producing
39 **treated with contempt (p. 273)**
41 "...Always give yourselves fully __ the work of the Lord..." (1 Cor. 15:58)
42 "__ you not know that the wicked will not inherit the kingdom of God..." (1 Cor. 6:9)
43 "...the gift of God is eternal life __ Christ Jesus our Lord." (Rom. 6:23)
44 in no way
45 "...this is ____ the LORD says: You have not obeyed me..." (Jer. 34:17)
47 specific people

DOWN

2 "Consider him who endured such opposition ____ sinful men..." (Heb. 12:3)
4 allow, permit, agree to
5 **wind, breath, God the Holy Spirit (p. 331)**
6 "What benefit did you reap __ that time from the things you are now ashamed of..." (Rom. 6:21)
7 persons
8 "He who sows wickedness reaps trouble, and the rod of his fury will __ destroyed." (Prov. 22:8)
9 chance, occasion
12 that man; that person
14 "Those ___ belong to Christ Jesus have crucified the sinful nature..." (5:24)
16 **household (p. 284)**
17 **scatters seed (p. 372); plants**
18 "Sow ___ yourselves righteousness..." (Hos. 10:12)
19 **fallen human character (p. 363)**
21 **harvests (p. 194)**
22 **those of the faith, those who trust (p. 314)**
23 opposite of no
26 every
27 **led astray, caused to wander; deluded (p. 326)**
28 everlasting, unending
30 **harvest (p. 194)**
32 crop, produce
33 "...it is time __ seek the LORD..." (Hos. 10:12)
35 **profitable, generous, beneficial, upright, virtuous (p. 2)**
38 **the one true God (p. 193)**
39 male adult; person
40 not at all, in no way, absolutely not
45 you and I
46 like

Galatians 6:7-10

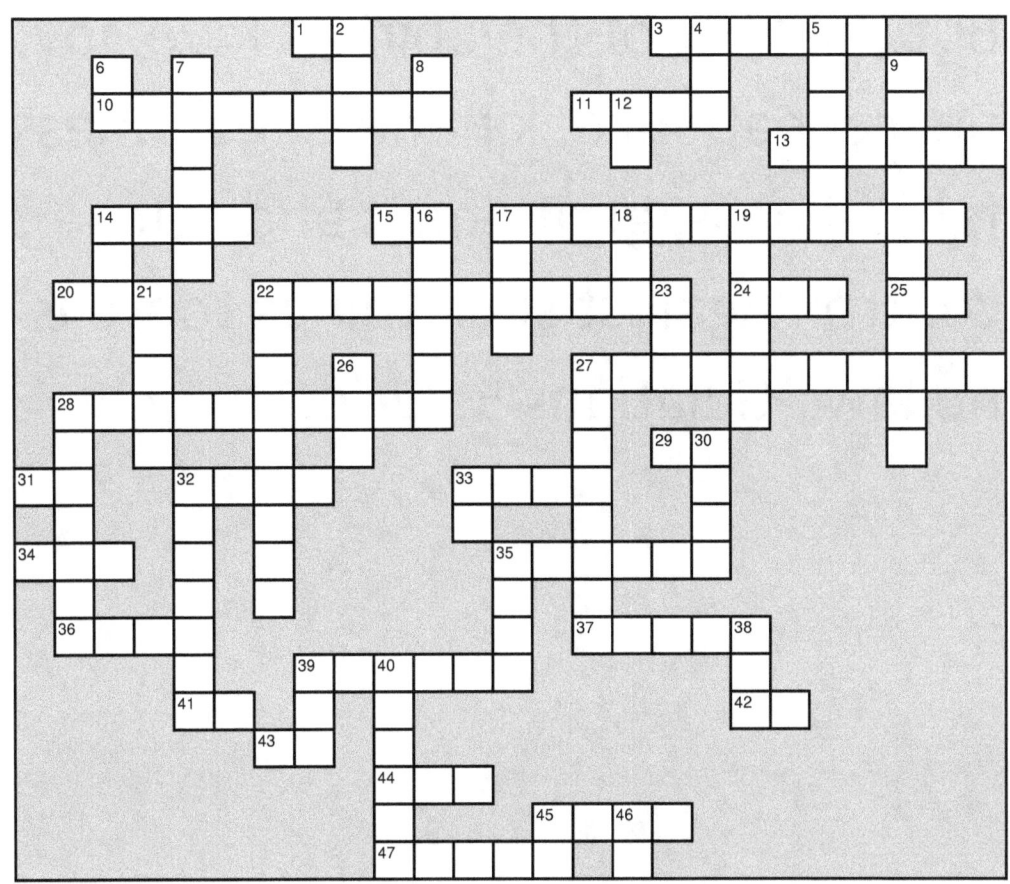

__ __ __ ____ : ____ be ____ . A __ __
2   3   2   8   3   6   3   5

__ __ __ . __ __ __ sows __ his
4   2   4   3   3   3   2   6

_____ , __ __ __ __ __ _____ ; the
12 (2 words) 4   4   6   4   4   11

one who sows __ please the ___ , from the Spirit will reap __ __ __ .
              2   6   7   4   3

__ not _____ __ __ __ , __ __ the __ __
2   11 (2 words) 2   5   4   3   2   6   4

__ will reap a ___ __ __ do not _____ . ___ , __ we __
2   7   2   2   6 (2 words) 9   2   4

_____ , let us do good to __ __ , ___ to __ who belong
11   3   6   10   5

to the __ __ ___ .
        6   2   9

But the fruit of the Spirit is love, joy, peace, patience, kindness, goodness, faithfulness, gentleness and self-control. Against such things there is no law. Galatians 5:22-23

Galatians 6:11

```
R U S E E H X Y R T U S L
I A Y R J J P B S D N O L
S F W R I T E I T H A S E
T U H I C I S U F A B I T
O Y G N U R S O T N R P T
B O A O E Q E S N D U A E
U U M P L I E T U S N T R
L B E B E O H P U S O E S
L A R G E L L O W N I R P
S R Y K Q U M I A B D T Y
U T O S A M R E A S O I R
F A Q U A Y T U S P R U T
W I T H M O T H Y W H A T
```

AS	MY	TO	WITH
HAND	OWN	USE	WRITE
LARGE	SEE	WHAT	YOU
LETTERS			

___ ___ ___ ___ ⁱ___ ___
 3   4   5   7   3   2

ⁱ___ ___ ___ ___ ___
  5   2   3   4   2   3

___.
 4

93

Galatians 6:12-16

ACROSS

1 **harmony, tranquility; safety, welfare, health (p. 119)**
5 and not
7 yours and mine
8 "...First clean the inside of the cup and dish, and then the outside also will ___ clean." (Mat. 23:26)
9 "Circumcision has value if you observe ___ law..." (Rom 2:25)
12 "...by their hypocrisy ____ Barnabas was led astray." (2:13)
13 in no way
14 **regulations, principles; the first five books of the Scriptures, or any single command of the Scriptures (p. 279)**
15 **body with a focus on the sinful human nature (p. 363)**
17 "For it is...we ___ worship by the Spirit of God..." (Phil. 3:3)
18 standard
19 put to death by being nailed to a cross
23 **pity; moral quality of feeling compassion and especially of showing kindness toward someone in need (p. 131)**
25 keep, mind, follow, comply with
26 "...You are like whitewashed tombs, _____ look beautiful on the outside but on the inside are full of dead men's bones... (Mat. 23:27)
27 absolutely not, not ever
29 not participating in the surgical process that was originally the sign of the covenant between Abraham and God
31 "...We died to sin; how can we live __ it any longer? (Rom. 6:2)
32 "Carry each other's burdens, and in ____ way you will fulfill the law of Christ. (6:2)
35 cause, motive, basis, explanation
37 **rapidly pursued, followed, or pressed (p. 104)**
38 "...let us __ good to all people..." (6:10)
39 "___ we know that our old self was crucified with him..." (Rom. 6:6)
41 *"he struggles with God;"* **nation that descended from Jacob (p. 203)**
43 **Joshua,** *"Yahweh saves"* **(p. 200)**
44 but, instead
47 "Woe __ you, teachers of the law and Pharisees, you hypocrites!..." (Mat. 23:25)
48 those people
49 **the one true God (p. 193)**
50 I, myself
51 **brag; rejoice, glory (p. 226)**
53 "...you welcomed me as if I were __ angel of God..." (4:14)
54 "For I resolved __ know nothing while I was

ACROSS (Continued)

with you except Jesus Christ and him crucified." (1 Cor. 2:2)
55 one point, a single factor

DOWN

2 apart from, not including, aside from
3 **force (p. 21)**
4 "...You clean the outside of the cup and dish, but inside they ___ full of greed and self-indulgence." (Mat. 23:25)
5 not
6 "...if you break the law, you have become as though you had not ____ circumcised. (Rom. 2:25)
7 **on the outside of the body (p. 364)**
10 everyone
11 keep away from, evade, prevent
13 opposite of old
15 **walk in, frame your conduct (p. 377)**
16 "...so that the body __ sin might be done away with..." (Rom. 6:6)
19 have or had the surgical process that was originally the sign of the covenant between Abraham and God
20 matters, is important, makes a difference
21 "to whom be glory for ____ and ever. Amen." (1:5)
22 concerning, regarding,
23 signifies
24 created thing
28 surgical process that was originally the sign of the covenant between Abraham and God
30 **Anointed One, Messiah, Son of David, Jesus who came to bring liberty from sin and peace with God and who will come again to bring all things under his control (p. 439)**
33 **appearance (p. 175)**
34 **crucifixion, wooden instrument used for a violent death (p. 374)**
36 one, single
40 "For it __ we who are the circumcision..." (Phil. 3:3)
42 **master (p. 244)**
45 attempting
46 "...If anyone else thinks he ___ reasons to put confidence in the flesh, I have more:" (Phil. 3:4)
49 **profitable, generous, beneficial, upright, virtuous (p. 2)**
50 might, could, possibly will
52 "...___ old has gone, the new has come!" (2 Cor. 5:17)
53 also, likewise

Galatians 6:12-16

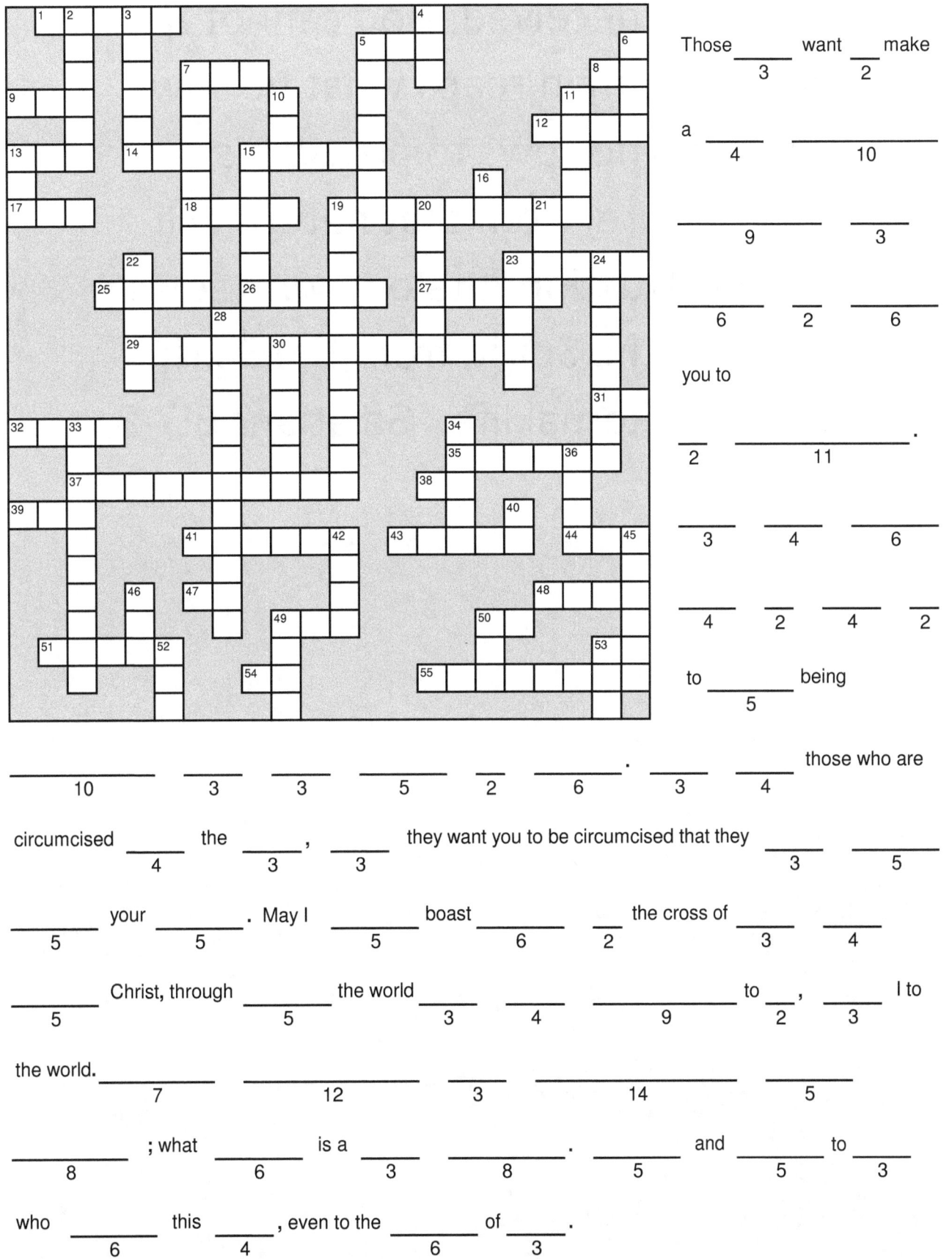

Do not be deceived: God cannot be mocked. A man reaps what he sows. The one who sows to please his sinful nature, from that nature will reap destruction; the one who sows to please the Spirit, from the Spirit will reap eternal life. Galatians 6:7-8

Galatians 6:17-18

ACROSS

- 4 lastly, in conclusion
- 7 bother, difficulty
- 10 **fellow countrymen, neighbors; fellow believers in the family of faith; regularly refers to men and women (p. 6)**
- 11 belonging to me
- 14 "The grace of the Lord Jesus Christ __ with your spirit…" (Phil. 4:23)
- 16 **master (p. 244)**
- 17 **soul, person's thoughts and feelings (p. 331)**
- 18 bring about, promote
- 19 I, myself

DOWN

- 1 "Are they servants __ Christ?…" (2 Cor. 11:23)
- 2 "…another will write __ his hand, 'The LORD'S,'" (Is. 44:5)
- 3 **Anointed One, Messiah, Son of David, Jesus who came to bring liberty from sin and peace with God and who will come again to bring all things under his control (p. 439)**
- 5 **the truth; most certainly, so be it (p. 18)**
- 6 belonging to you
- 8 carry, endure, suffer
- 9 yours and mine
- 10 human structure
- 11 **brands, burns (p. 376)**
- 12 **Joshua, "*Yahweh saves*" (p. 200)**
- 13 **kindness and favor toward someone (p. 433)**
- 15 "___ just as the sufferings of Christ flow over into our lives, so also through Christ our comfort overflows." (2 Cor. 1:5)
- 16 allow

_____, _____ no one _____ _____ _____, _____ I _____ _____ _____
  7   3   5   2   7   3   4   2   2

_____ the _____ _____ _____. The _____ of _____ _____ Jesus _____ _____
  4   5   2   5   5   3   4   6   2

with _____ _____, _____. _____.
     4   6   8   4

Lord willing, the book of James is next…keep a watchful eye.

Galatians in the New International Version

Chapter 1

Paul, an apostle—sent not from men nor by a man, but by Jesus Christ and God the Father, who raised him from the dead— ² and all the brothers and sisters with me,

To the churches in Galatia:

³ Grace and peace to you from God our Father and the Lord Jesus Christ, ⁴ who gave himself for our sins to rescue us from the present evil age, according to the will of our God and Father, ⁵ to whom be glory for ever and ever. Amen.

No Other Gospel

⁶ I am astonished that you are so quickly deserting the one who called you by the grace of Christ and are turning to a different gospel— ⁷ which is really no gospel at all. Evidently some people are throwing you into confusion and are trying to pervert the gospel of Christ. ⁸ But even if we or an angel from heaven should preach a gospel other than the one we preached to you, let them be eternally condemned! ⁹ As we have already said, so now I say again: If anybody is preaching to you a gospel other than what you accepted, let them be eternally condemned!

¹⁰ Am I now trying to win the approval of men, or of God? Or am I trying to please men? If I were still trying to please men, I would not be a servant of Christ.

Paul Called by God

¹¹ I want you to know, brothers, that the gospel I preached is not something that man made up. ¹² I did not receive it from any man, nor was I taught it; rather, I received it by revelation from Jesus Christ.

¹³ For you have heard of my previous way of life in Judaism, how intensely I persecuted the church of God and tried to destroy it. ¹⁴ I was advancing in Judaism beyond many Jews of my own age and was extremely zealous for the traditions of my fathers. ¹⁵ But when God, who set me apart from birth and called me by his grace, was pleased ¹⁶ to reveal his Son in me so that I might preach him among the Gentiles, I did not consult any man, nor did I go up to Jerusalem to see those who were apostles before I was, but I went immediately into Arabia and later returned to Damascus.

¹⁸ Then after three years, I went up to Jerusalem to get acquainted with Peter and stayed with him fifteen days. ¹⁹ I saw none of the other apostles—only James, the Lord's brother. ²⁰ I assure you before God that what I am writing you is no lie. ²¹ Later I went to Syria and Cilicia. ²² I was personally unknown to the churches of Judea that are in Christ. ²³ They only heard the report: "The man who formerly persecuted us is now preaching the faith he once tried to destroy." ²⁴ And they praised God because of me.

Chapter 2

Paul Accepted by the Apostles

Fourteen years later I went up again to Jerusalem, this time with Barnabas. I took Titus along also. ² I went in response to a revelation and set before them the gospel that I preach among the Gentiles. But I did this privately to those who seemed to be leaders, for fear that I was running or had run my race in vain. ³ Yet not even Titus, who was with me, was compelled to be circumcised, even though he was a

Greek. ⁴ This matter arose because some false believers had infiltrated our ranks to spy on the freedom we have in Christ Jesus and to make us slaves. ⁵ We did not give in to them for a moment, so that the truth of the gospel might remain with you.

⁶ As for those who seemed to be important—whatever they were makes no difference to me; God does not judge by external appearances—those men added nothing to my message. ⁷ On the contrary, they saw that I had been entrusted with the task of preaching the gospel to the Gentiles, just as Peter had been to the Jews. ⁸ For God, who was at work in the ministry of Peter as an apostle to the Jews, who was also at work in my ministry as an apostle to the Gentiles. ⁹ James, Peter and John, those reputed to be pillars, gave me and Barnabas the right hand of fellowship when they recognized the grace given to me. They agreed that we should go to the Gentiles, and they to the Jews. ¹⁰ All they asked was that we should continue to remember the poor, the very thing I was eager to do.

Paul Opposes Peter

¹¹ When Peter came to Antioch, I opposed him to his face, because was clearly in the wrong. ¹² Before certain men came from James, he used to eat with the Gentiles. But when they arrived, he began to draw back and separate himself from the Gentiles because he was afraid of those who belonged to the circumcision group. ¹³ The other Jews joined him in his hypocrisy, so that by their hypocrisy even Barnabas was led astray.

¹⁴ When I saw that they were not acting in line with the truth of the gospel, I said to Peter in front of them all, "You are a Jew, yet you live like a Gentile and not like a Jew. How is it, then, that you force Gentiles to follow Jewish customs?

¹⁵ "We who are Jews by birth and not 'Gentile sinners' ¹⁶ know that a man is not justified by observing the law, but by faith in Jesus Christ. So we, too, have put our faith in Christ Jesus that we may be justified by faith in Christ and not by observing the law, because by observing the law no one will be justified.

¹⁷ "If, while we seek to be justified in Christ, it becomes evident that we ourselves are sinners, does that mean that Christ promotes sin? Absolutely not! ¹⁸ If I rebuild what I destroyed, I prove that I am a lawbreaker. ¹⁹ "For through the law I died to the law so that I might live for God. ²⁰ I have been crucified with Christ and I no longer live, but Christ lives in me. The life I live in the body, I live by faith in the Son of God, who loved me and gave himself for me. ²¹ I do not set aside the grace of God, for if righteousness could be gained through the law, Christ died for nothing!"

Chapter 3

Faith or Observance of the Law

You foolish Galatians! Who has bewitched you? Before your very eyes Jesus Christ was clearly portrayed as crucified. ² I would like to learn just one thing from you: Did you receive the Spirit by observing the law, or by believing what you heard? ³ Are you so foolish? After beginning with the Spirit, are you now trying to attain your goal by human effort? ⁴ Have you suffered so much for nothing—if it really was for nothing? ⁵ Does God give you his Spirit and work miracles among you because you observe the law, or because you believe what you heard?

⁶ Consider Abraham: "He believed God, and it was credited to him as righteousness." ⁷ Understand, then, that those who believe are children of Abraham. ⁸ The Scripture foresaw that God would justify the Gentiles by faith, and announced the gospel in advance to Abraham: "All nations will be blessed through you." ⁹ So those who have faith are blessed along with Abraham, the man of faith.

¹⁰ All who rely on observing the law are under a curse, for it is written: "Cursed is everyone who does not continue to do everything written in the Book of the Law." ¹¹ Clearly no one who is justified before God by the law, because, "The righteous will live by faith." ¹² The law is not based on faith; on the contrary, "The man who does these things will live by them." ¹³ Christ redeemed us from the curse of the law by becoming a curse for us, for it is written: "Cursed is everyone who is hung on a tree." ¹⁴ He redeemed us in order that the blessing given to Abraham might come to the Gentiles through Christ Jesus, so that by faith we might receive the promise of the Spirit.

The Law and the Promise

¹⁵ Brothers, let me take an example from everyday life. Just as no one can set aside or add to a human covenant that has been duly established, so it is in this case. ¹⁶ The promises were spoken to Abraham and to his seed. The Scripture does not say "and to seeds," meaning many people, but "and to your seed," meaning one person, who is Christ. ¹⁷ What I mean is this: The law, introduced 430 years later, does not set aside the covenant previously established by God and thus do away with the promise. ¹⁸ For if the inheritance depends on the law, then it no longer depends on a promise; but God in his grace gave it to Abraham through a promise.

¹⁹ What, then, was the purpose of the law? It was added because of transgressions until the Seed to whom the promise referred had come. The law was put into effect through angels by a mediator. ²⁰ A mediator, however, does not represent just one party; but God is one.

²¹ Is the law, therefore, opposed to the promises of God? Absolutely not! For if a law had been given that could impart life, then righteousness would certainly have come by the law. ²² But the Scripture declares that the whole world is a prisoner of sin, so that what was promised, being given through faith in Jesus Christ, might be given to those who believe.

²³ Before this faith came, we were held prisoners by the law, locked up until the faith should be revealed. ²⁴ So the law was put in charge to lead us to Christ that we might be justified by faith. ²⁵ Now that this faith has come, we are no longer under the supervision of the law.

Sons of God

²⁶ You are all sons of God through faith in Christ Jesus, ²⁷ for all of you who were baptized into Christ have clothed yourselves with Christ. ²⁸ There is neither Jew nor Greek, slave nor free, male nor female, for you are all one in Christ Jesus. ²⁹ If you belong to Christ, then you are Abraham's seed, and heirs according to the promise.

Chapter 4

What I am saying is that as long as the heir is a child, he is no different from a slave, although he owns the whole estate. ² He is subject to guardians and trustees until the time set by his father. ³ So also, when we were children, we were in slavery under the basic principles of the world. ⁴ But when the time had fully come, God sent his Son, born of a woman, born under the law, ⁵ to redeem those under the law, that we might receive the full rights of sons. ⁶ Because you are his sons, God sent the Spirit of his Son into our hearts, the Spirit who calls out, *"Abba*, Father." ⁷ So you are no longer a slave, but a son; and since you are a son, God has made you also an heir.

Paul's Concern for the Galatians

⁸ Formerly, when you did not know God, you were slaves to those who by nature are not gods. ⁹ But now that you know God—or rather are known by God—how is it that you are turning back to those

weak and miserable principles? Do you wish to be enslaved by them all over again? ¹⁰ You are observing special days and months and seasons and years! ¹¹ I fear for you, that somehow I have wasted my efforts on you.

¹² I plead with you, brothers, become like me, for I became like you. You have done me no wrong. ¹³ As you know, it was because of an illness that I first preached the gospel to you. ¹⁴ Even though my illness was a trial to you, you did not treat me with contempt or scorn. Instead, you welcomed me as if I were an angel of God, as if I were Christ Jesus himself. ¹⁵ What has happened to all your joy? I can testify that, if you could have done so, you would have torn out your eyes and given them to me. ¹⁶ Have I now become your enemy by telling you the truth?

¹⁷ Those people are zealous to win you over, but for no good. What they want is to alienate you from us, so that you may be zealous for them. ¹⁸ It is fine to be zealous, provided the purpose is good, and to be so always and not just when I am with you. ¹⁹ My dear children, for whom I am again in the pains of childbirth until Christ is formed in you, ²⁰ how I wish I could be with you now and change my tone, because I am perplexed about you!

Hagar and Sarah

²¹ Tell me, you who want to be under the law, are you not aware of what the law says? ²² For it is written that Abraham had two sons, one by the slave woman and the other by the free woman. ²³ His son by the slave woman was born in the ordinary way; but his son by the free woman was born as the result of a promise.

²⁴ These things may be taken figuratively, for the women represent two covenants. One covenant is from Mount Sinai and bears children who are to be slaves: This is Hagar. ²⁵ Now Hagar stands for Mount Sinai in Arabia and corresponds to the present city of Jerusalem, because she is in slavery with her children. ²⁶ But the Jerusalem that is above is free, and she is our mother. ²⁷ For it is written:

"Be glad, O barren woman,
    who bears no children;
break forth and cry aloud,
    you who have no labor pains;
because more are the children of the desolate woman
    than of her who has a husband."

²⁸ Now you, brothers, like Isaac, are children of promise. ²⁹ At that time the son born in the ordinary way persecuted the son born by the power of the Spirit. It is the same now. ³⁰ But what does Scripture say? "Get rid of the slave woman and her son, for the slave woman's son will never share in the inheritance with the free woman's son." ³¹ Therefore, brothers, we are not children of the slave woman, but of the free woman.

Chapter 5

Freedom in Christ

It is for freedom that Christ has set us free. Stand firm, then, and do not let yourselves be burdened again by a yoke of slavery.

² Mark my words! I, Paul, tell you that if you let yourselves be circumcised, Christ will be of no value to you at all. ³ Again I declare to every man who lets himself be circumcised that he is obligated to obey the whole law. ⁴ You who are trying to be justified by the law have been alienated from Christ; you have

fallen away from grace. ⁵ But by faith we eagerly await through the Spirit the righteousness for which we hope. ⁶ For in Christ Jesus neither circumcision nor uncircumcision has any value. The only thing that counts is faith expressing itself through love.

⁷ You were running a good race. Who cut in on you and kept you from obeying the truth? ⁸ That kind of persuasion does not come from the one who calls you. ⁹ "A little yeast works through the whole batch of dough." ¹⁰ I am confident in the Lord that you will take no other view. The one who is throwing you into confusion will pay the penalty, whoever he may be. ¹¹ Brothers, if I am still preaching circumcision, why am I still being persecuted? In that case the offense of the cross has been abolished. ¹² As for those agitators, I wish they would go the whole way and emasculate themselves!

Life by the Spirit

¹³ You, my brothers, were called to be free. But do not use your freedom to indulge the sinful nature; rather, serve one another in love. ¹⁴ The entire law is summed up in a single command: "Love your neighbor as yourself." ¹⁵ If you keep on biting and devouring each other, watch out or you will be destroyed by each other.

¹⁶ So I say, live by the Spirit, and you will not gratify the desires of the sinful nature. ¹⁷ For the sinful nature desires what is contrary to the Spirit, and the Spirit what is contrary to the sinful nature. They are in conflict with each other, so that you do not do what you want. ¹⁸ But if you are led by the Spirit, you are not under the law.

¹⁹ The acts of the sinful nature are obvious: sexual immorality, impurity and debauchery; ²⁰ idolatry and witchcraft; hatred, discord, jealousy, fits of rage, selfish ambition, dissensions, factions ²¹ and envy; drunkenness, orgies, and the like. I warn you, as I did before, that those who live like this will not inherit the kingdom of God.

²² But the fruit of the Spirit is love, joy, peace, patience, kindness, goodness, faithfulness, ²³ gentleness and self-control. Against such things there is no law. ²⁴ Those who belong to Christ Jesus have crucified the sinful nature with its passions and desires. ²⁵ Since we live by the Spirit, let us keep in step with the Spirit. ²⁶ Let us not become conceited, provoking and envying each other.

Chapter 6

Doing Good to All

Brothers, if someone is caught in a sin, you who are spiritual him gently. But watch yourself, or you also may be tempted. ² Carry each other's burdens, and in this way you will fulfill the law of Christ. ³ If anyone thinks he is something when he is nothing, he deceives himself. ⁴ Each one should test his own actions. Then he can take pride in himself, without comparing himself to somebody else, ⁵ for each one should carry his own load.

⁶ Anyone who receives instruction in the word must share all good things with his instructor.

⁷ Do not be deceived: God cannot be mocked. A man reaps what he sows. ⁸ The one who sows to please his sinful nature, from that nature will reap destruction; the one who sows to please the Spirit, from the Spirit will reap eternal life. ⁹ Let us not become weary in doing good, for at the proper time we will reap a harvest if we do not give up. ¹⁰ Therefore, as we have opportunity, let us do good to all people, especially to those who belong to the family of believers.

Not Circumcision but the New Creation

[11] See what large letters I use as I write to you with my own hand!

[12] Those who want to make a good impression outwardly are trying to compel you to be circumcised. The only reason they do this is to avoid being persecuted for the cross of Christ. [13] Not even those who are circumcised obey the law, yet they want you to be circumcised that they may boast about your flesh. [14] May I never boast except in the cross of our Lord Jesus Christ, through which the world has been crucified to me, and I to the world. [15] Neither circumcision nor uncircumcision means anything; what counts is a new creation. [16] Peace and mercy to all who follow this rule, even to the Israel of God.

[17] Finally, let no one cause me trouble, for I bear on my body the marks of Jesus. [18] The grace of our Lord Jesus Christ be with your spirit, brothers. Amen.

Answer Key

Galatians 1:1-5

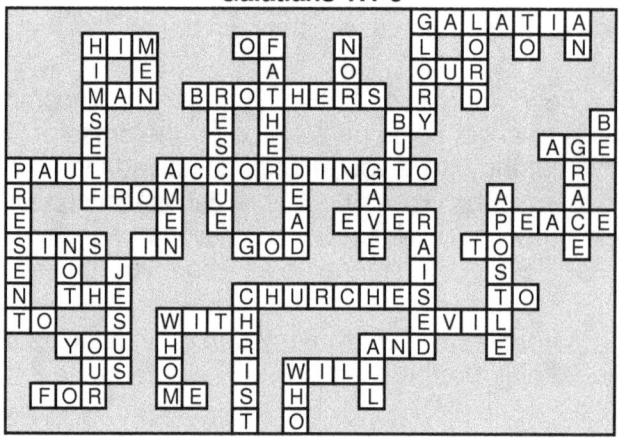

Galatians 1:6-9

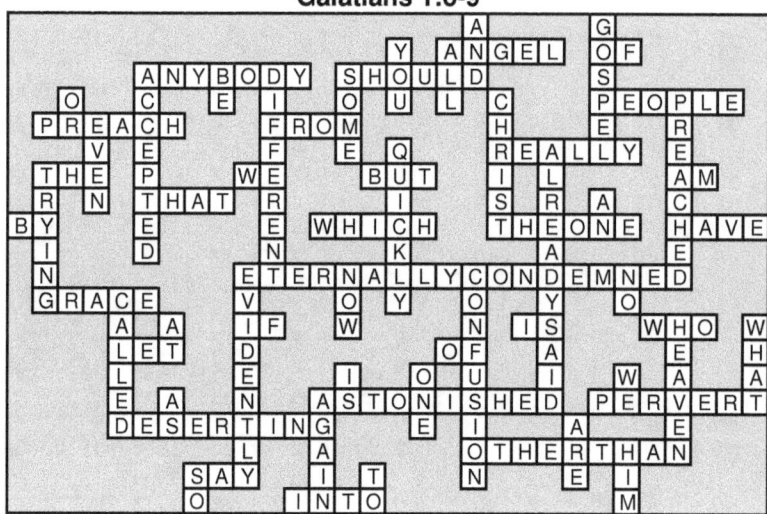

Galatians 1:10

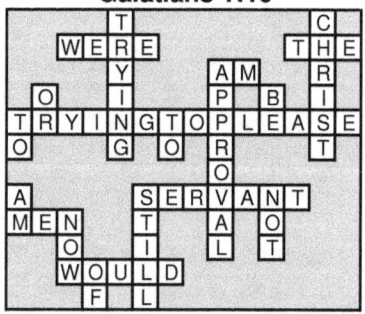

Galatians 1:11-12

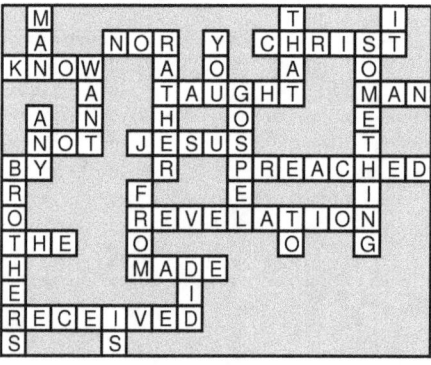

104

Galatians 1:13-17

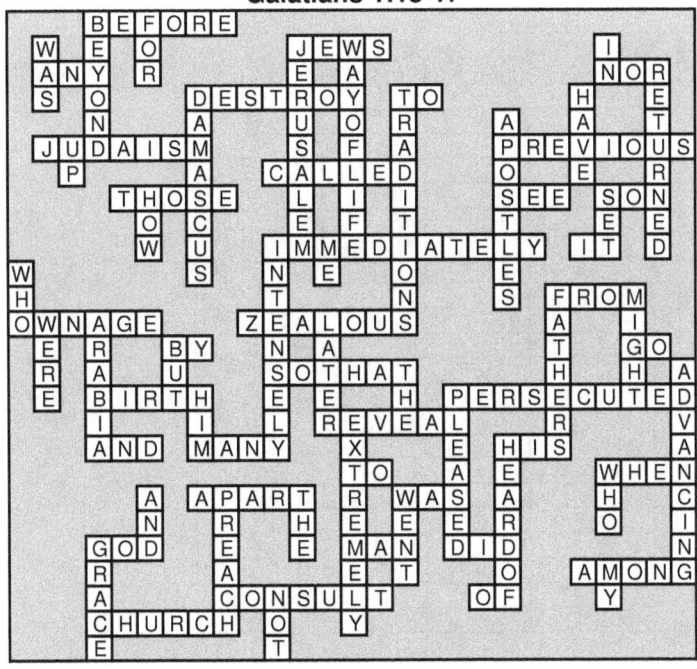

Galatians 1:18-24

Galatians 2:1-5

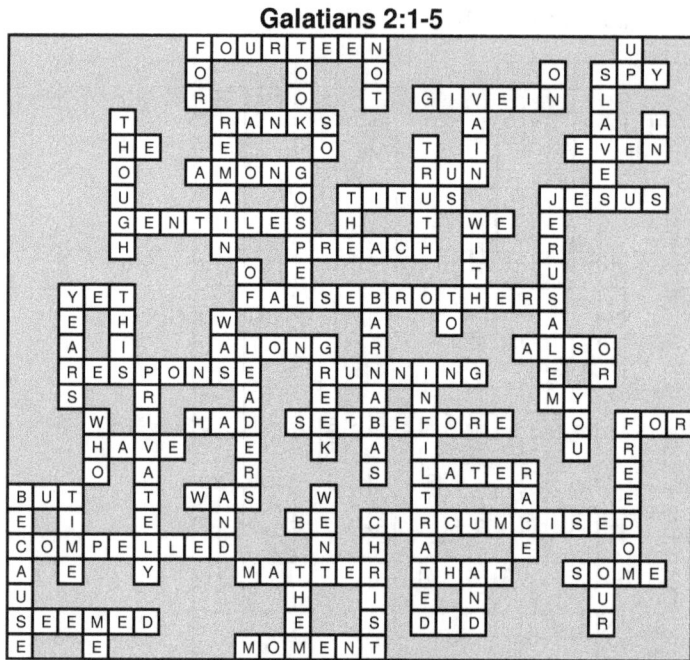

Galatians 2:6-10

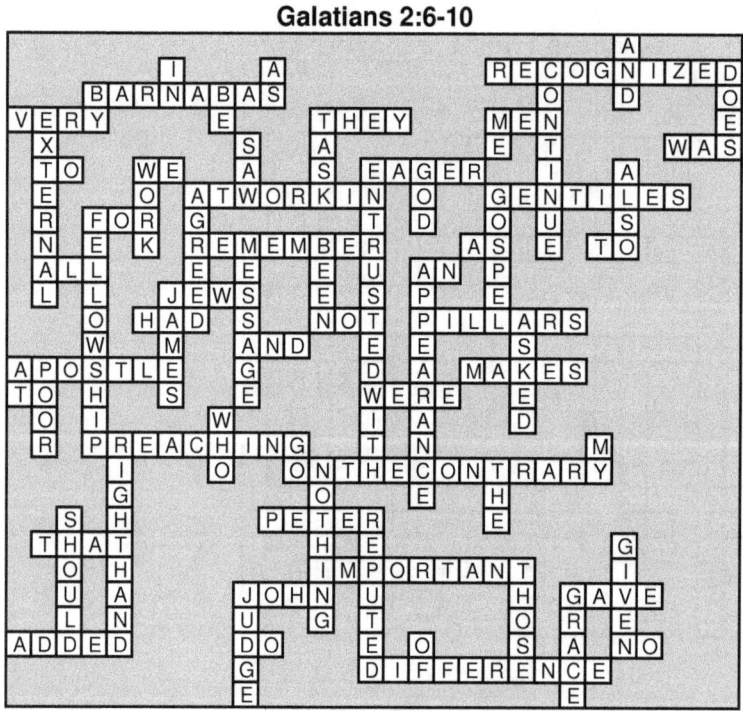

Galatians 2:11-13

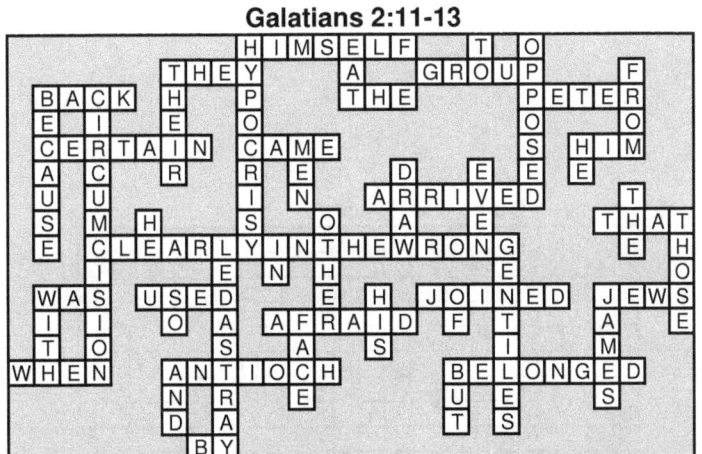

Galatians 2:14

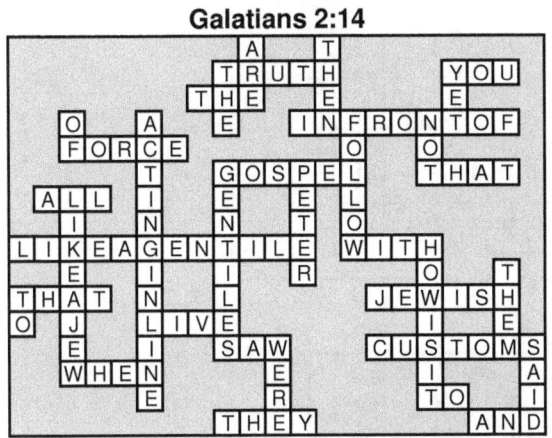

Galatians 2:15-16

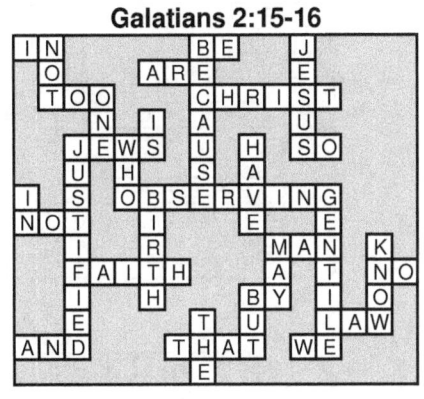

Galatians 2:17-21

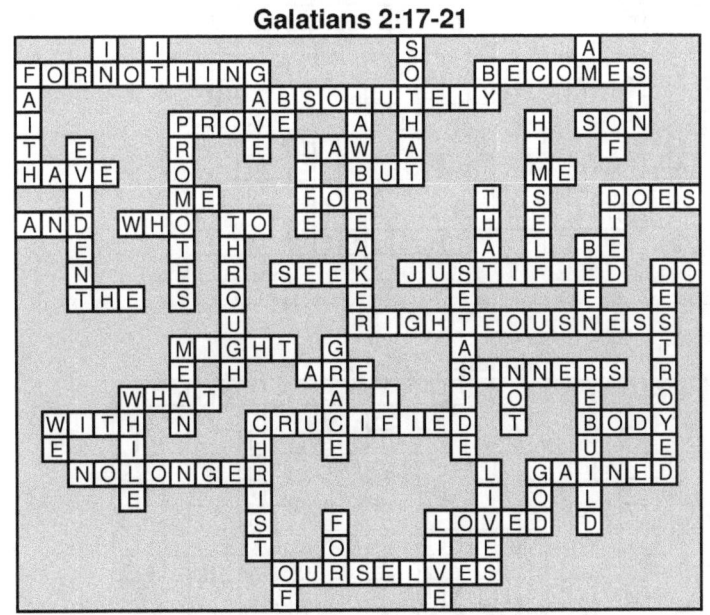

Galatians 3:1-5

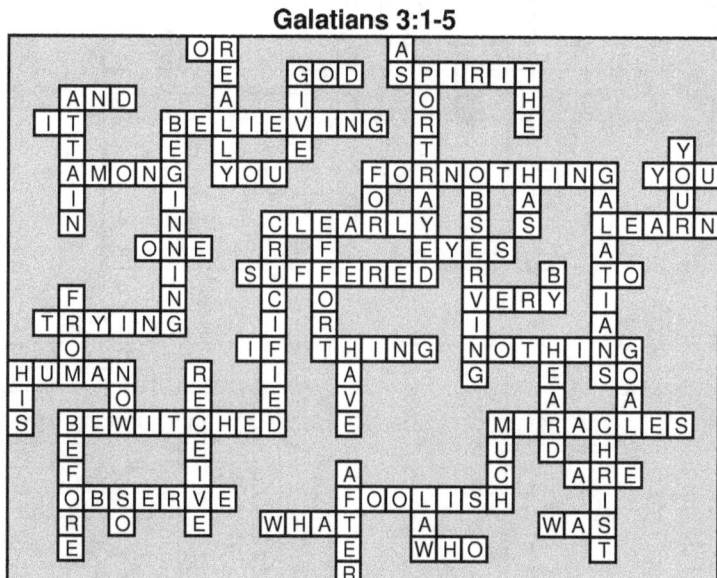

Galatians 3:6-9

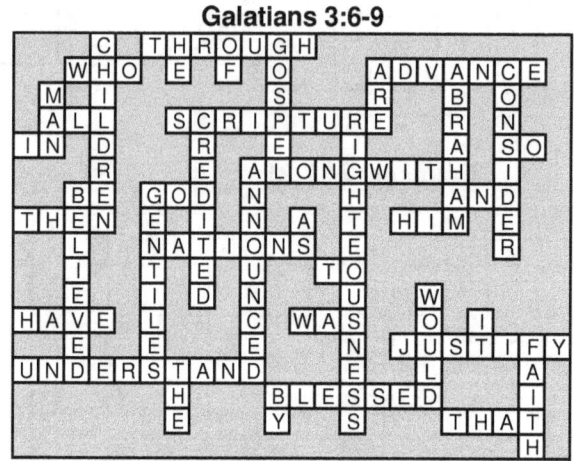

Galatians 3:10-14

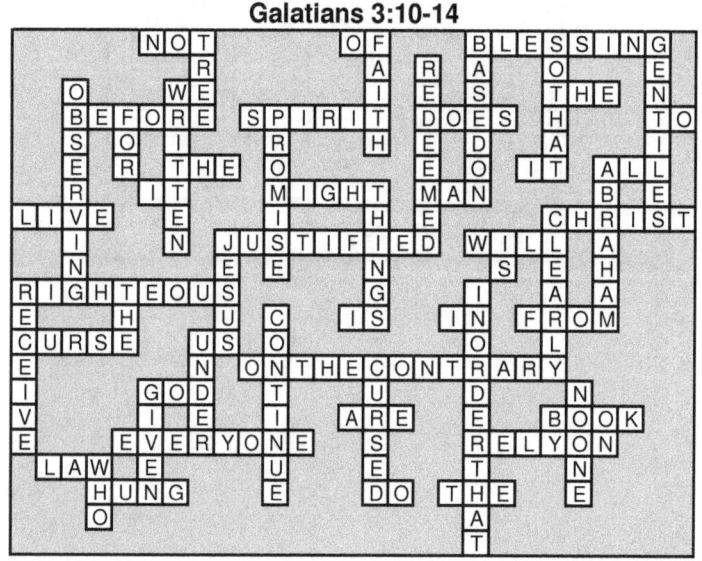

Galatians 3:15-18

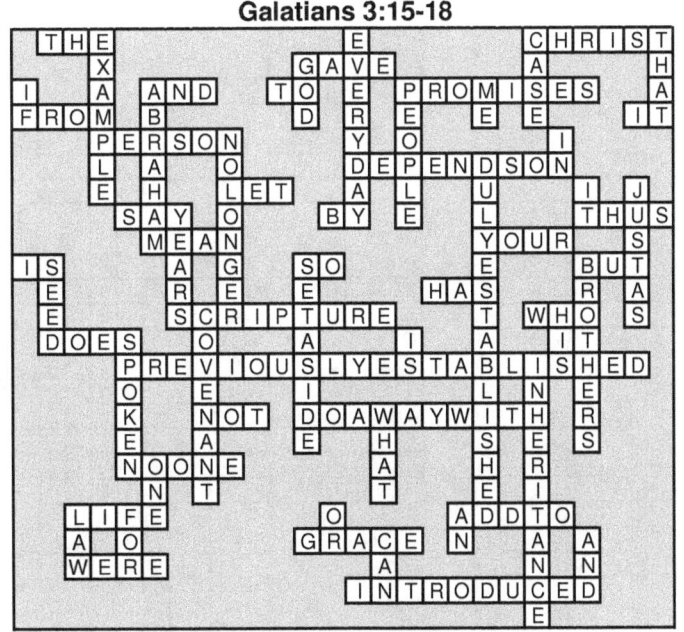

Galatians 3:19-20

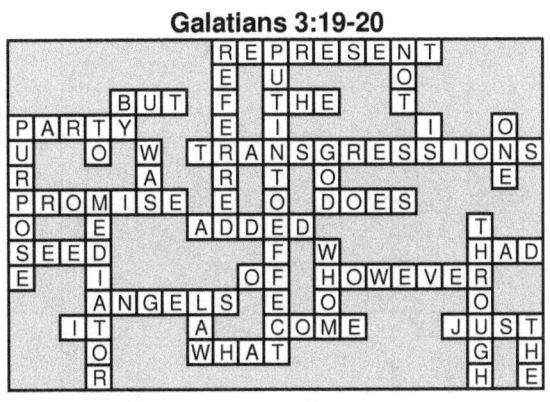

Galatians 3:21-22

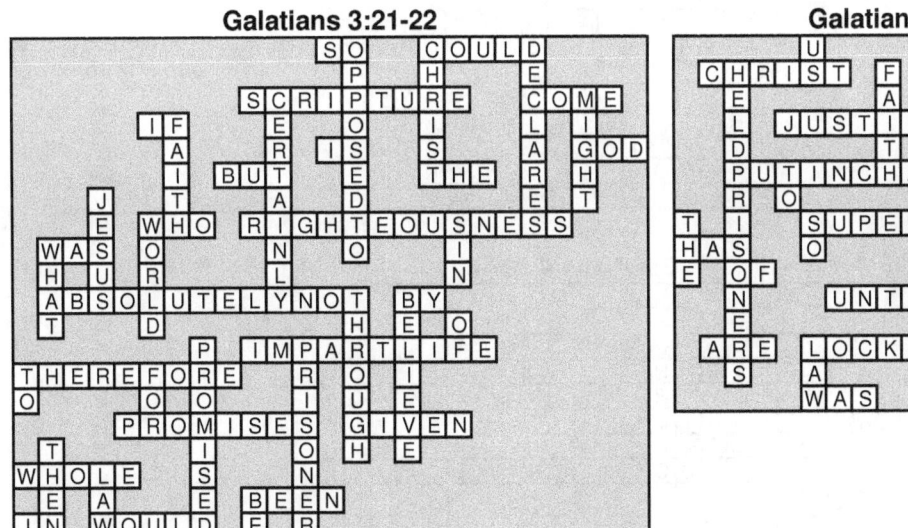

Galatians 3:23-25

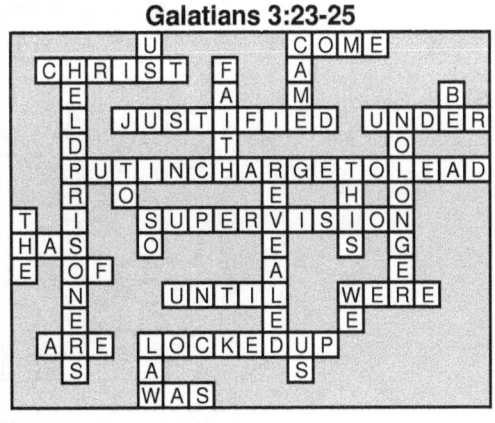

Galatians 3:26-29

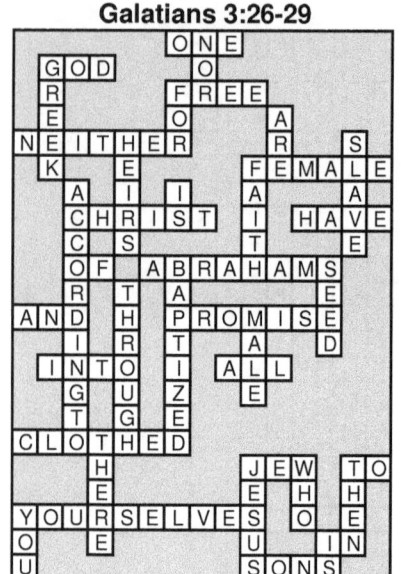

Galatians 4:1-7

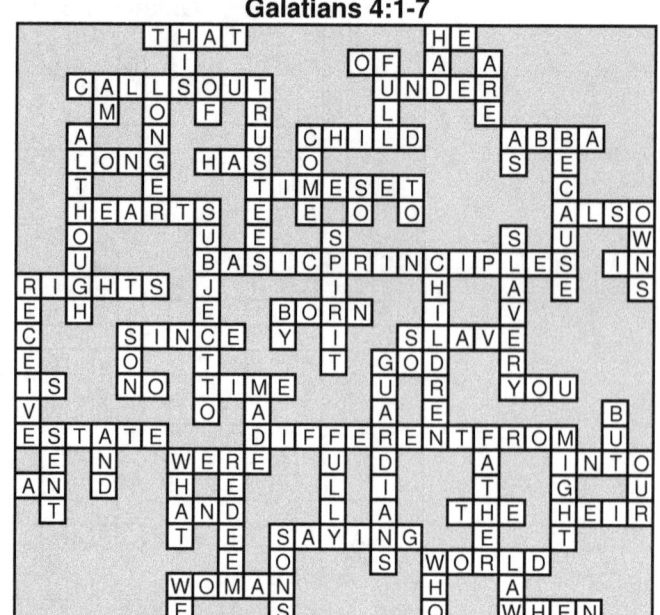

Galatians 4:8-11

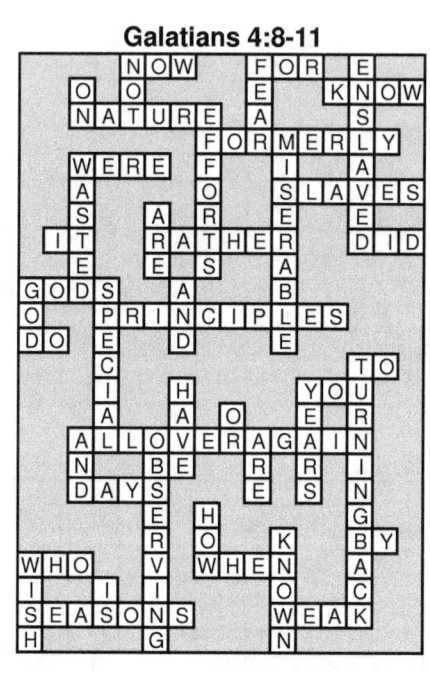

Galatians 4:12-16

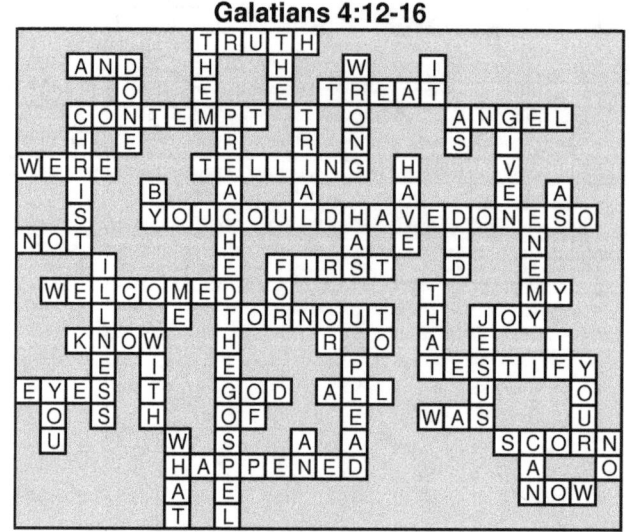

Galatians 4:17-20

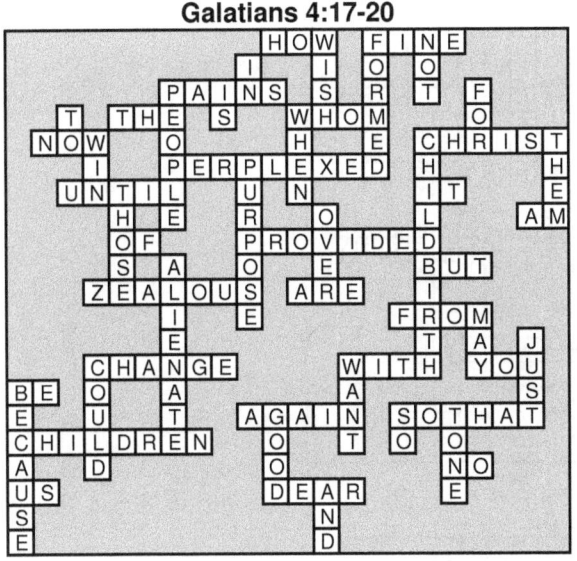

Galatians 4:21-23

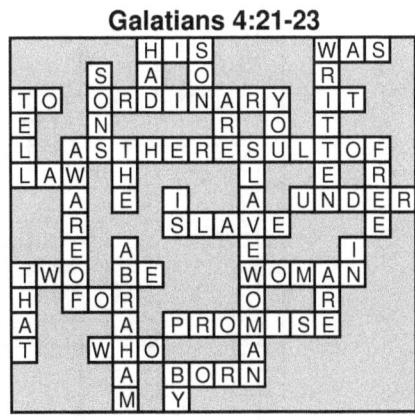

Galatians 4:24-27

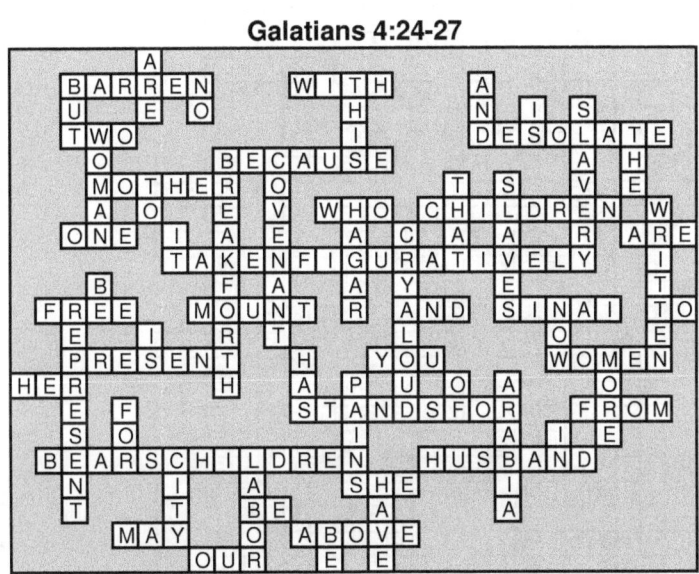

Galatians 4:28-31

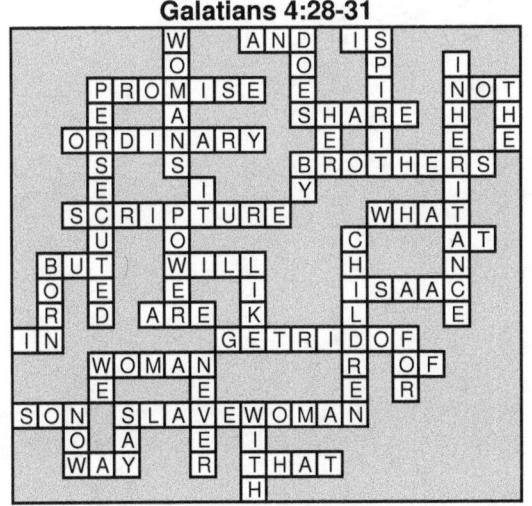

Galatians 5:1

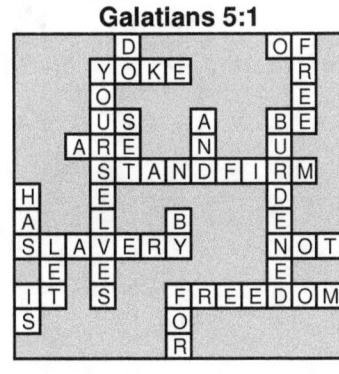

Galatians 5:2-6

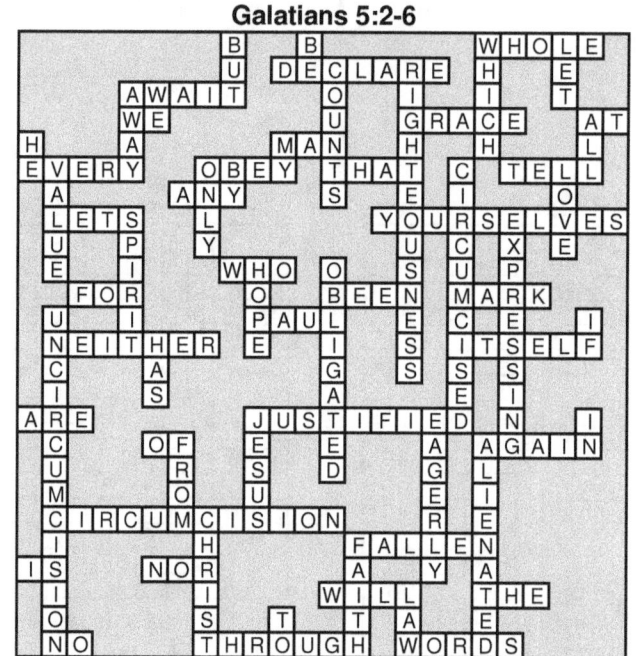

Galatians 5:7-12

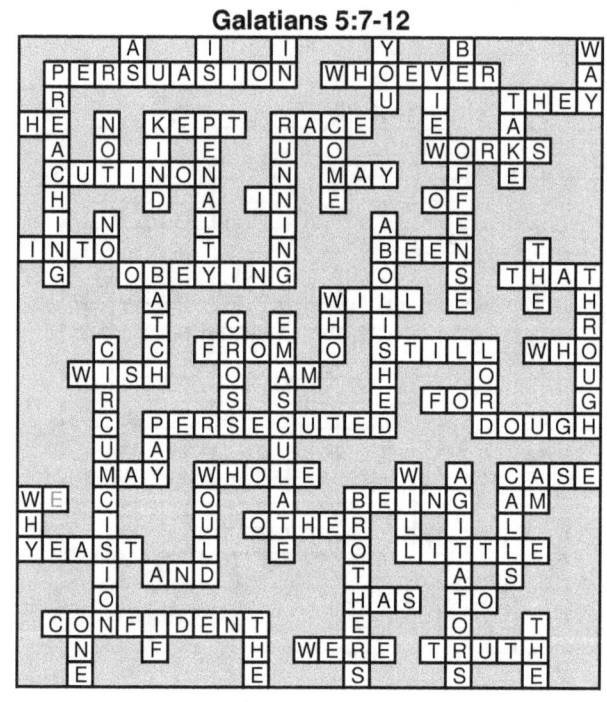

Galatians 5:13-15

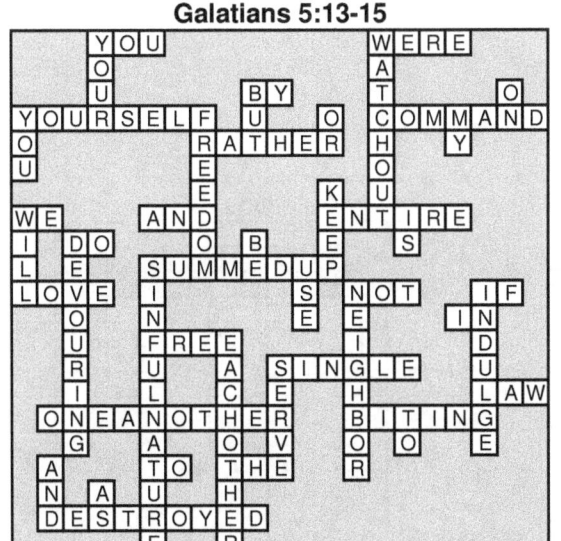

Galatians 5:16-18

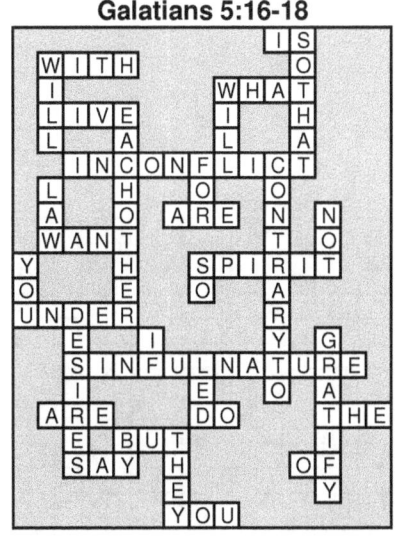

Galatians 5:19-21

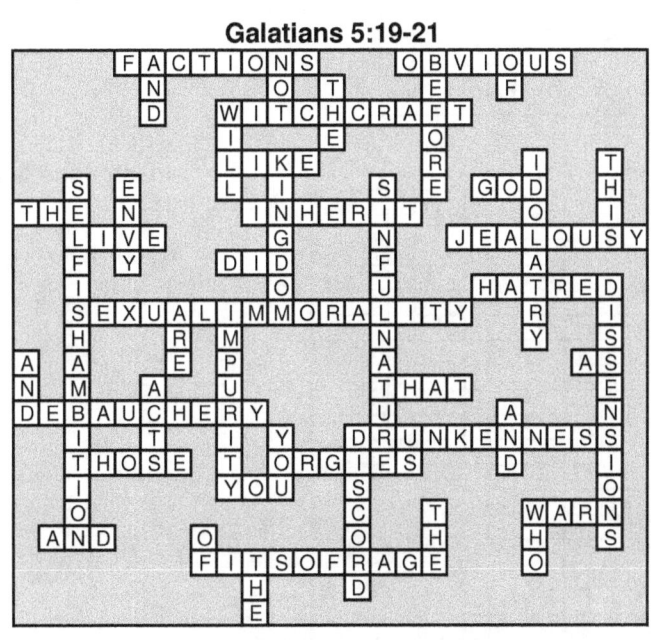

Galatians 5:22-26

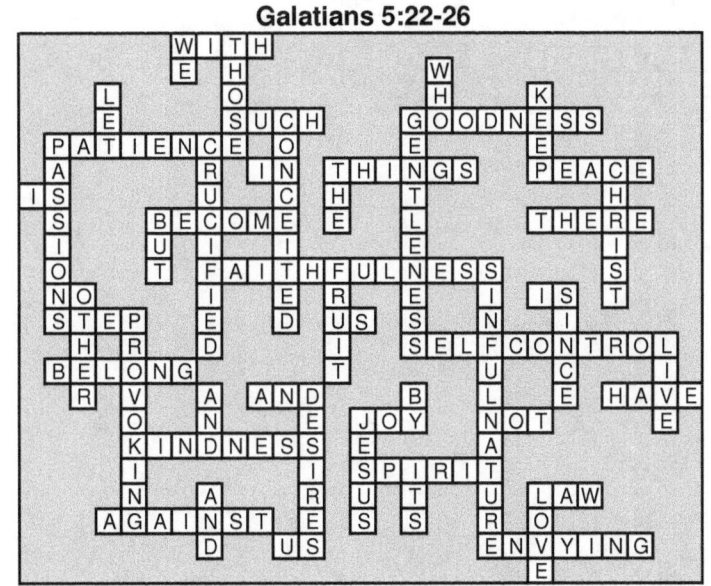

Galatians 6:1-5

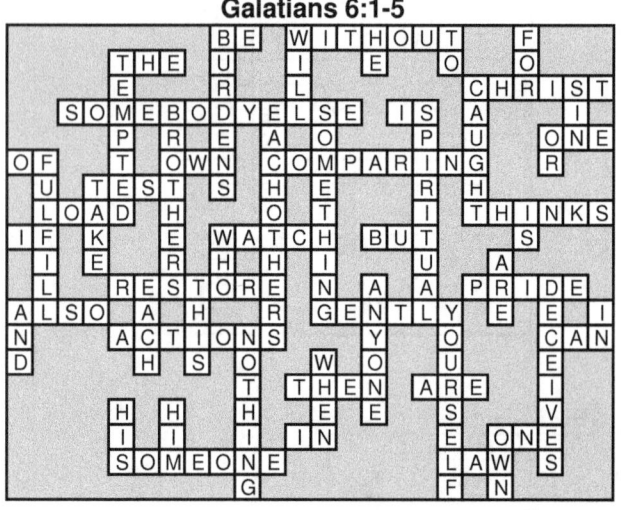

Galatians 6:6

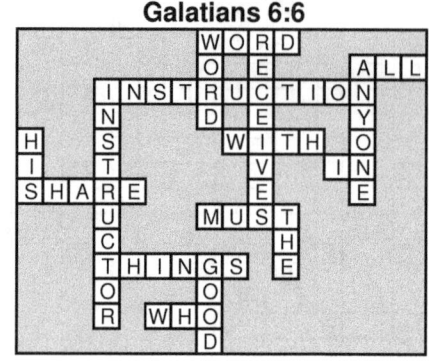

Galatians 6:7-10

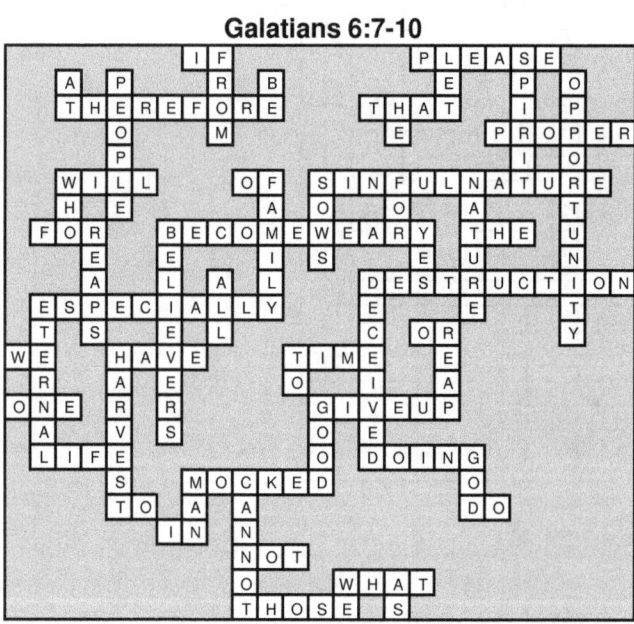

Galatians 6:11

```
R B S̶ E̶ E̶ H X Y R T U S L
I A Y R J J P B S D N O L
C F W̶ R̶ I̶ T̶ E̶ I T H A S E
T U H I C I S U F A B I T
O Y G N U R S O T N R P T
B O A O E Q E S N D U A E
U U M P L I E T U S N T R
L B E B E O H P U̶ S̶ E̶ P S
L̶ A̶ R̶ G̶ E̶ L L O̶ W̶ N I R P
S R Y K Q U M I A B D T Y
U T O D A M R E A S O I R
F A Q U A Y T U S P R U T
W̶ I̶ T̶ H̶ M O T H Y W̶ H̶ A̶ T̶
```

Galatians 6:12-16

Galatians 6:17-18

www.ingramcontent.com/pod-product-compliance
Lightning Source LLC
Chambersburg PA
CBHW081332230426
43667CB00018B/2908